A Coming of God into Time and History

The Theological Project of M-D Chenu OP

InterfaceTheology:
Incorporating *Sapientia et Sciencia* and in association with *Wort und Antwort* (Germany)
Volume 7, Number 2, 2021

Subscription rates
Print Local: Individual Aus $55, Institutions Aus $65.
Overseas: Individuals US $60, Institutions US $65.

Interface Theology is a biannual refereed journal of theology published in print, Epub and PDF by ATF Press Publishing Group.
The journal is a scholarly ecumenical and interdisciplinary publication, aiming to serve the church and its mission, promoting a broad-based interpretation of Christian theology within a trinitarian context, encouraging dialogue between Christianity and other faiths, and exploring the interface between faith and culture. It is published in English for an international audience.

ISSN 2203-465X
Cover art work Yvonne Ashby

ISBN: 978-1-922737-29-8   soft
         978-1-922737-30-4   hard
         978-1-922737-31-1   epub
         978-1-922737-32-8   pdf

THEOLOGY

An imprint of ATF Theology part of the ATF Press Publishing Group which is owned by
ATF (Australia) Ltd.
PO Box 234,
Brompton, SA, 5007
Australia
www.atfpress.com
Making a lasting impact

A Coming of God into Time and History

The Theological Project of M-D Chenu OP

Edited by Hilary D Regan

THEOLOGY

2021

Table of Contents

InterfaceTheology 7/2 2021

Editorial

There is a similarity in how Thomas Aquinas (1225 to 1274) was a student of Albert the Great (1200 to 1280) but wrote more and was more widely known and recognised as a significant theologian than his teacher, and how Yves Congar (1904 to 1995) was connected to Marie-Dominique Chenu (1895 to 1900). As Thomas was a student of Albert's, so Congar was a student of Chenu's. Both students wrote and had more published works than their teacher's and both became more widely known, through their writings. But there are differences in the relationship between Albert and Thomas and the relationship between Congar and Chenu. Chenu's writings were included on the Index of forbidden books within the Catholic Church[1] before any of Congar's (beginning with Chenu's *Une École de théologie: Le Saulchoir.*) and the two were more collaborators and colleagues than Albert and Thomas by the very fact that they were both considered by the Vatican as among the 'unorthodox' of theologians of their time more so than was the case of Albert and Thomas.

Chenu did not have the same manner as Congar of writing diaries/journals of what was occurring around him along the way as did Congar. Both taught at the Saulchoir for many years, first in Belgium

---

1. This occurred in February 1942. On the other hand, Congar was restricted from writing for a number of years and his *Vraie et fausse réforme dans l'Église* (*True and False Reform in the Church*) was forbidden by Rome in 1950 and then prevented from teaching and writing by Rome (along with others), but his writings were not put on the Index in same way as Chenu's Ecole Saulchior.

and then when it returned to France and lived in the same Convents (Priory) for much of their Dominican religious life.[2]

Chenu's and Congar's lives did not follow exactly the same trajectory (for example, Chenu did not serve in the army in World War II as did Congar), but their lives were connected theologically in many ways in the *novelle théologie* (New Theology), which had its origins in the Dominican House of Studies (*Studium*) Le Saulchoir,[3] where they both taught and worked together[4], in the *Une école de théologie: Le Saulchoir* book,[5] and in other writings over the years. It was Congar who wrote of Chenu, in a dedication of a book he was working on, 'To Marie Dominique CHENU, Friend, Teacher, Brother'.[6]

Chenu was, like Congar, involved in the deliberations of the Second Vatican Council, but not to the same extent or degree as Congar and his diary of the Council is a much smaller volume.[7] However his influence in the Council was significant.

---

2. In 1903 the Dominicans were expelled from France and moved their place for studies to Kain, Belgium, in what was a former Cistercian monastery called *Le Saulchoir*. In 1939 they returned to the France, in Étiolles, giving it still the name *Le Saulchoir* and in 1971 to Paris, where in 1992 the *Centre d'études du Saulchoir* was established.

3. A book entitled the *Saulchoir Affair* (translated from French) by Etienne Fouiloux will be published by ATF Theology in 2021 which examines factors to the lead up to Chenu's book being put on the Index.

4. Congar says of Chenu of their time together: '(we) chatted open-heartedly and in freshness of what for me were discoveries and first perceptions. We fell into profound agreement. Respecting both this mission ['that our generation's mission was to bring to effect within the Church, that which was true in the queries and the problems posed by modernism'], and the necessity of 'wiping out baroque theology'. Yves Congar, *Journal of a Theologian 1946–1956*, translated by Denis Minns (Adelaide: ATF Theology, 2015), 36–37.

5. The book, *Une école de théologie: Le Saulchoir*, was based on a lecture given by Chenu at *Le Saulchoir* as Regent of Studies (head of studies) for the Dominicans in the Province to which he belonged (one which has had different names over time, Province of Paris, Province of France), and was originally published internally as a small booklet in 1937. In 1938 he was called to Rome about the book and thus began a period of investigation into the book and *Le Saulchoir*, as outlined in Fouiloux's book. A translation into English of the *Une école de théologie: Le Saulchoir* book, together with various other documents, will be published by ATF Theology in 2021.

6. Congar, *Journal of a Theologian 1946–1956*, 74.

7. See *Vatican II Notebook: A Council Journal, 1962–1963*, Marie-Dominique Chenu; critical edition and introduction by Alberto Melloni, translated by Paul

Chenu was, like Congar, engaged with the Jocist movements, founded by Joseph Cardijn in Belgium. Congar wrote an extensive volume on the vocation of the laity,[8] while some would consider Chenu was more deeply involved on a day to day level with the workers movement than Congar.[9]

This volume of essays is a study of Chenu; his times and his work. It comes after a similar volume was published by ATF Theology on Congar in 2019,[10] and after another volume, also published by ATF Theology on the French Dominicans, including Chenu and Congar in 2019.[11] It would be the hope that one day a book could be devoted to each of the other Dominicans in that volume (Sertilange, Lebret, Loew, Liége and Couturier), with studies on their respective theological work along with some writings by each. Each, like Congar and Chenu, made a significant contribution to theology in the twentieth century, each in very different spheres.

What follows in this volume, however, are papers by writers from Germany (Ulrich Engel, OP x 2), the USA (Thomas O'Meara, OP) and Australia (Janette Gray, RSM) on Chenu and on his work and theological project. Unlrich Engel has two pieces, the first situates historically and theologically the *novelle theologie* and Chenu's work. The second article is a translation of a German article Chenu's basic theological instincts and gives the background and central emphases of the *Une école de théologie: Le Saulchoir*. O'Meara's piece is an examination of Chenu's work as theologian and historian and who 'saw the *Summa theologiae* as a source for new ideas and ministerial movements'. Janette Gray's piece is chapter 2 of her *M-D Chenu's Christian Anthropology: Nature and Grace in Society and Church*. That chapter, along with all other chapters in the book used extensive quotation from original French sources of Chenu's work. For this work

---

Philibert (Adelaide: ATF Theology, 2015), 174 pages as opposed to Congar's *My Journal of the Council* (Adelaide: ATF Theology, 2015), translated by Mary John Ronayne OP, Cecily Boulding OP, English editor Denis Minns OP, 1040 pages.

8.   Yves Congar, *Lay People in the Church* (London: Geoffrey Chapman, 1965).
9.   For a full examination of Chenus' theology see Jannette Gray, *M-D Chenu's Christian Anthropology: Nature and Grace in Society and Church* (Adelaide: ATF Theology, 2019), chapter 2 on 'Chenu's Theological Project' is in this volume.
10. *Congar and Chenu: Friend, Teacher, Brother* (Adelaide: ATF Theology, 2019).
11. *Scanning the Signs of the Times: French Dominicans in the Twentieth Century*, Thomas O'Meara and Paul Philibert (Adelaide: ATF Theology, 2013).

the French text remain but underneath each there is an English tar-nation. The volume finishes with a piece by Chenu himself that was originally published in 1939, of which no original French text can be found at this stage. The piece appeared as 'Catholic Action and the Mystical Body' in a volume written by Paul McGuire and John Fitzsimons entitled *Restoring all Things: A Guide to Catholic Action.*[12]

Congar and Chenu labored to make known widely the Pauline theology of church community and the organic ecclesiology of it the German theologian Johann Adam Möhler. These presentations of the church as a living organism with a variety of activities, of charisms and ministries, have had an influence on the development today of the ecclesiology of synodality.

Hilary Regan
Adelaide
November 2021

---

12. *Restoring All Things: A Guide to Catholic Action* (London: Sheed and Ward, 1939), 1–15.

InterfaceTheology 7/2 2021

The Question of Modernity in Catholic Theology. The Dispute over 'Nouvelle Théologie' as the Context of M-D Chenu's Book Une École de théologie: Le Saulchoir (1937)[1]

Ulrich Engel, OP[2]

Introduction

The term *'nouvelle théologie'* (New Theology) is a battle term.[3] At least, that was the case for a large part of the twentieth century; more exactly, the period between the middle of the 1930s and the Second Vatican Council (1962–1965). The term *nouvelle théologie* first surfaced in 1948. An article about new trends in theology appeared in the semi-official Vatican newspaper *l'Osservatore Romano* on 10 February 1948. The author of this article, Mgr Pietro Parente, later chosen to be a cardinal, described a French variant of the theology of that time, a variant which had been objected to by Rome since 1936, as *nouvelle théologie*.[4] In the following period, *nouvelle théologie* became the accepted term used to describe this particular theological trend.

---

1. Translated from German by Bonifatius Hicks, OP.
2. Ulrich Engel OP, born 1961 in Düsseldorf, studied Münster, Bonn and Benediktbeuern in Germany and Fribourg in Switzerland. In 1984, he joined the Dominican Order, and is currently director of the 'Institut M.-Dominique Chenu' (www.institut-chenu.eu), and editor of the theological periodical 'Wort und Antwort' (www.wort-und-antwort.de). He is also Regent of Studies of the 'Province of Teutonia' of the Dominican Order (www.dominikaner.de), and is teaching Fundamental Theology at the 'Philosophisch-Theologische Hochschule Münster' (www.pth-muenster.de). He has published various books and articles on the theology of the Dominican Order, the Political Theology of Johann Baptist Metz, theological aesthetics, and the points of meeting of philosophy and theology. He lives in Berlin.
3. *Cf* Ulrich Engel, 'El debate en torno a la 'nueva teología'. Una comprobación histórico-teológica en perspectiva dominicana', in *Ciencia Tomista*, 97 (2006): 125–140.
4. *Cf* Pietro Parente, 'Nuove tendenze teologiche', in *L'Osservatore Romano*, 10.2.1942.

After a few introductory comments my text will examine four areas of thought: First, I will outline the intellectual roots of the *nouvelle théologie*. The appropriate keywords in this are 'modernism' and 'neo-scholasticism'. In a second section, I will sketch the principal features of the *nouvelle théologie*. In this connection, the Dominican House of Studies at Le Saulchoir and its then Rector Marie-Dominique Chenu, OP, are of particular importance. This is because the theological controversy which was later traded under the name of *nouvelle théologie* began with a speech Chenu gave in 1936 at Le Saulchoir. An excursus on the influence of Henri-Dominique Lacordaire, OP, the refounder of the Dominicans in France, completes the second part. In the third section, I will consider the opponents of the *nouvelle théologie*; in this my particular interest is in the Dominican contribution. The central location of the criticism was the 'Angelicum', the university of the Dominican Order in Rome. In the fourth section my investigation is in historical theology, and I will take as my theme the rehabilitation of the *nouvelle théologie*, which implicitly took place through the Second Vatican Council. Here also, Chenu stands at the centre of my considerations.[5] And in the middle of this equally theological and political debate in the Catholic Church was—quasi as matrial object—the book 'Une école de théologie: Le Saulchoir'!

Intellectual Roots of the *Nouvelle Théologie*

Modernism

No theology falls straight from heaven: all theologies are historically dependent. Their coming into existence and their passing away are both situated in an historical context.

Looked at in terms of intellectual history, the great question in the nineteenth century was about *history*. For theology the question can be formulated as follows: How can a contingent (or particular, or limited, or chance) event of history gain universal (or general) significance? Put in other words: How do the so-called 'eternal truths' of the Christian faith beome incarnate in an history of the world and of humanity, one which is subject to continual change?

---

5. For the biographies of the Dominicans involved see *Dictionnaire biographique des frères prêcheurs. Dominicains des provinces françaises (XIXᵉ-XXᵉ siècles)*: https://journals.openedition.org/dominicains/ [15.05.2020].

At the beginning of the twentieth century, two attempts to answer this question competed againt each other. While one side propagated a strict *division* between faith and the world, the other side attempted to build a bridge between the two. The former position had its roots in the Council of Trent (1545–1563); this first Council of modern times had attempted to separate itself from modernity. The latter ecclesiastical position—so-called 'modernism' (incidentally, this word was originally an insult from the opposing side)—relied, in contrast, on *dialogue* with the modern world. This, in turn, provoked the opposing party to the so-called 'antimodernist' reactions.

It not surprising that the front line of these theological disputes was also mirrored within the Dominican Order. Otto Weiss, an historian who teaches in Rome, writes in his large-scale investigation of modernism and antimodernism in the Dominican Order that:

> It would be surprising if the storms of the so-called modernism at the beginning of the 20th century had blown over the Dominican Order without any effect. Especially, if one understands modernism not only as striving to be up-to-date [. . .], but rather enquires into its philosophical and theological objectives, the following thought forces itself upon us: an Order with the varied and often controversial tradition of the Dominicans could not ignore the questions raised by the 'modernists' as if they were not there. In some way or other, the members had to take a stand. And, in actual fact, we find Dominicans amongst the 'modernists' as well as the 'antimodernists'.[6]

One of the most prominent proponents of a theological discussion with modernity was the biblical scholar and founder of the École Biblique in Jerusalem, Marie-Joseph Lagrange OP (1855–1938). Lagrange wanted to rise to the challenge raised by the question of history in exegesis and biblical theology. So, he sought to explore the historical roots of the bible. Today, the historical-critical method of exegesis is quite usual. No student of theology can avoid it. Further, Lagrange paid attention to archaeology. All of this, however, brought about the criticism and reaction of the Vatican. In recognition of the

---

6. Otto Weiss, *Modernismus und Antimodernismus im Dominikanerorden. Zuglich ein Beitrag zum 'Sodalitum Pianum'*, Quellen und Studien zur neueren Theologiegeschichte, Volume 2 (Regensburg: Pustet, 1998), 5.

person and works of Lagrange, Swiss Old Testament scholar Herbert Haag has written:

> The coercive measures of Pius X [pope from 1903 until 1914; *Ulrich Engel*] [. . .] have caused immeasurable damage to Catholic biblical studies and have thrown them back a hundred years. The superficial blame for this goes to a false concept of tradition on the part of the Magisterium, which shows itself to be incapable of differentiating between historical and theological tradition, and, therefore, declared itself to be the competent authority on purely historical-critical questions. Lagrange was no disrespecter of tradition. But he refused to make tradition into an idol. Tradition must always be paired with progress: it requires continual reconsideration.[7]

Lagrange was certainly not alone in these matters. His position received fundamental support from the (Dominican) professors of exegesis at the theology faculty of the University of Fribourg in Switzerland. At the same time, however, there were antimodernists numbered among other Dominicans such as, for example, the German Dominican Albert Maria Weiss OP (1844–1925).[8] Otto Weiss (not related to the former) summarised his views by raguing that:

> The tensions which mirrored the upheaval in Church, theology, state and society, philosophy, science and culture at the turn of the century [meaning the end of the nineteenth century and the beginning of the twemntieth century; *Ulrich Engel*] met as if in a focal point at the priory in Fribourg in Üchtland. (. . .) At the centre of the disputes stood (. . .) the two basic trends of theology, the historical and the systematic. Both were cultivated by the Dominicans. Both clashed with each other during the period of the modernist crisis. In Fribourg, where 'modernists' [. . .] and 'antimodernists' [. . .]

---

7. Herbert Haag, 'Wider die Angst vor der Freiheit: Die Geschichte des Pioniers katholischer Bibelwissenschaft Marie-Joseph Lagrange (1855–1936)', *Gegenentwürfe. 24 Lebensläufe für eine andere Theologie*, edited by Hermann Häring and Karl-Josef Kuschel (München—Zürich: Piper, 1988), 269–281, here at 280f.

8. To the person of Albert M Weiss see Anton Landersdorfer, 'Albert Maria Weiss OP (1844–1925)', in *Antimodernismus und Modernismus in der katholischen Kirche. Beiträge zum theologiegeschichtlichen Vorfeld des II. Vatikanums*, edited by Hubert Wolf, Programm und Wirkungsgeschichte des II. Vatikanums Volume 2, (Paderborn *et al*: Schöningh, 1998), 195–216.

lived in the same priory, the battle about modernism was conducted at its fiercest as a struggle about the place of the bible and of biblical exegesis within theology.[9]

Neo-scholasticism

A second answer to the question of the way the Church dealt with modernity is represented in neo-scholasticism. The Lucerne dogmatic theologian Wolfgang W Müller OP explains:

> This movement, which was received in terms of the whole Church at Vatican I [1869/70] was about making classical scholasticism fruitful for the question of modernity. This theology sought to read that which is new with the eyes of the old.[10]

However much such a procedure—reading the contemporary with the eyes of and older merthod—is justified theologically, it is, nevertheless, problematic if it does not get used in reverse round as well—according to the maxim: read the old with the eyes of the new! Precisely this point of view was not welcome in many places, since it encouraged a 'mixing'—according to the charge brought against it—of old and new, of ecclesiastical tradition and modern society. Instead, there was an attempt to preserve a strict division between nature and grace and, thereby, of church and world, by latching onto baroque scholasticism by means of the old-fashioned model of a 'two-storey theory'. In the course of these efforts at separation, there was 'the development of a sort of separate society' in the Catholic Church, 'since, looked at in terms of the history of mentalities, the neo-scholastic movement represents an attempt to preserve the religious and cultural identity of Catholicism in the modern, pluralistic world'.[11] The price paid by the Church for this was too high: 'theology and history found themselves at the beginning of the [twentieth century] century in a sort of ghetto mentality, which implied a certain

---

9. Weiss, *Modernismus und Antimodernismus im Dominikanerorden*, 276.
10. Wolfgang W Müller, 'Was kann an der Theologie neu sein? Der Beitrag der Dominikaner zur "nouvelle théologie"', in *Zeitschrift für Kirchengeschichte*, 110 (1999): 86–104, here at 86f.
11. Müller, 'Was kann an der Theologie neu sein?', 87.

separation from other Christian churches, from society, and from their cultural and intellectual milieu'.[12]

Principal Features of the *Nouvelle Théologie*

The *nouvelle théologie* took up the challenge against the tendencies of separatism and criticism of the world which have just been outlined. The new theological movement had its origins in France and in the French-speaking part of Belgium.

In this connection, the French Dominicans had been leading the way not only in theology but also in pastoral work since the end of the 1920s. Their activities and advances were soon examined and reported on very critically, such as, for example, the historical reading of St Thomas (in contravention of the official method of reading him, in which only the 'eternal truths' would be filtered out of it), their closeness to the Christian workers' youth movement, ecumenical involvement and, later, sympathy and closeness to the worker priest's movement.[13]

It was certainly no coincidence that it was French Dominicans who, at least in the first instance, put their mark on the *nouvelle théologie*. For, 'in the nineteenth century, the Dominican Order in France had a religious whose life's work, the refounding of the Order in France, increasingly raised up the topics of the position of the Church and theology in modern society'[14]: Henri-Dominique Lacordaire.

Excursus: Henri-Dominique Lacordaire OP (1802–1861)

Let us go back to Paris in the year 1848: Lacordaire had by then been a Dominican for nine years.[15] As a young diocesan priest, he

---

12. Müller, 'Was kann an der Theologie neu sein?', 87.
13. *Cf* Johannes Bunnenberg, 'In den Fängen des Hl. Offiziums. "Die düsteren Jahre" des Dominikaners Yves Congar', in *Wort und Antwort,* 44/1 (2003): 19–24.
14. Müller, 'Was kann an der Theologie neu sein?', 90. On the historical classification of this period in connection with the Province of Francia *cf.* Guy Bedouelle, 'Les provinces dominicaines de la langue française en Europe au XIXe et XXe siècle', *Mémoire Dominicaine,* No 9/1996, 41–50.
15. Introductions in German to the person and work of Lacordaire: Thomas Eggensperger and Ulrich Engel, *Dominikanerinnen und Dominikaner. Geschichte und Spiritualität,* (Kevelaer: Topos, 2010), 96–107; Franz Müller, 'Henri-Dominique Lacordaire (1802–1861). Existenz zwischen den Fronten', in *Wort und Antwort,* 30/2 (1989): 58–63.; Urban Plotzke, *Pater Lacordaire. Ein Zeuge für die Freiheit. 1802–1861,* (Köln *et al*: Amerikanisch-Ungarischer Verlag, 1961).

had already made a name for himself in France—for example, as a preacher in Notre Dame. Christoph Martin describes the scene as follows:

> The success which he [Lacordaire] had in Notre Dame and in the large towns of France was overwhelming. There were almost 10,000 listeners, of all ages, but especially youth, bishops and politicians, students and noble ladies, artists and intellectuals, Protestants and non-believers, who all came together in front of his pulpit. The so-called 'conferences', which could last several hours, began around noon; the churches began to fill at 5 o'clock in the morning. In his series of sermons, which he continued for almost two decades, he expounded the whole of the faith [. . .] They were, we could say, dogmatic sermons, based on scripture and tradition. Lacordaire did not teach any new theology, but the way in which he expounded classical doctrines was completely new. Not the usual moralising theological jargon, but a new language, full of pictures and often surprising thoughts, always lively and open for the inspiration of the moment, addressing the feelings and the understanding of his listeners. His preaching instructed in the faith and always had, at the same time, the unbeliever or the opponent in its sights, explaining, deepening, defending and fighting.[16]

After an interruption caused by his joining the Order of Preachers, Lacordaire took up again his preaching activities in Notre Dame in 1841. In a sermon of 1848 with the title 'About the human being as a social being'[17] he took argued that which is generally referred to as 'society' is at the same time both natural and willed by God: 'Both of these things are completely true, society is natural for people, but nevertheless it has a divine origin.'[18] Lacordaire had to defend his the-

---

16. Christoph-M Martin, 'Henri-Dominique Lacordaire. Ein Mann seiner Zeit', *Dominikanerinnen und Dominikaner. Lebensbilder aus dem Predigerorden*, edited by Franz Müller, Grosse Ordensleute Vollume 3 (Fribourg: Kanisius—Konstanz: Kanisiuswerk, 1988), 98–112, here at 107f.

17. The German translation used as the basis for the quotations here is: Henri-Dominique Lacordaire, *Die Kanzelvorträge in der Notre-Dame-Kirche zu Paris*. Translated from French into German by Joseph Lutz and JA Hitzfelder, Volume 3: Vorträge von 1848, 1849 und 1950 (Tübingen: Laupp, 1851), 169–193.

18. Lacordaire, *Die Kanzelvorträge in der Notre-Dame-Kirche zu Paris*, 180.

ses against those who 'maintain that society is a purely human institution, and, going even further, an institution which is against nature.'[19] Lacordaire insisted on the indisputable connection of both of the aspects, the social (human) and the natural (divine), against the dualistic attitude of those who tended to permanently divide these: 'The human being is [. . .] social, as a result of his natural arrangement; he is naturally gregarious, and, therefore, also naturally social.'[20]

Beginning with the thesis that the social constitution of the human being is deeply willed by God, Lacordaire declared that all Christians have a social responsibility. The Christian is required not to retreat into a dreamy romanticism in an apparently ideal alternative world, but to productively form the real and concrete environment. This task is both a political and a cultural responsibility.

The Dominican House of Studies Le Saulchoir

The location of the Dominican contribution to the *nouvelle théologie* was the Dominican House of Studies at Le Saulchoir—at that time in Belgium for political reasons. From here, the Dominicans participated in an epochal historical upheaval, which shook the theoretical foundations of the Church and of theology and precipitated a general change of mentality.[21] Johannes Bunnenberg OP describes the situation at that time as follows:

> The theological monopoly of neo-scholasticism in the Church, its style of exercising power, the way it seals itself off from the rest of the world—all of these are called into question. The topics which are discussed have arisen through the delay in coming to terms with modernity: It is a question of the historicity of perception, of the structures and of the

---

19. Lacordaire, *Die Kanzelvorträge in der Notre-Dame-Kirche zu Paris*, 173.
20. Lacordaire, *Die Kanzelvorträge in der Notre-Dame-Kirche zu Paris*, 180.
21. For the best presentation on the historical genesis and the pastoral-theological effects of Chenu's 'Une école de théologie: Le Saulchoir' see Christian Bauer, *Ortswechsel der Theologie M.-Dominique Chenu im Kontext seiner Programmschrift 'Une école de théologie: Le Saulchoir'* (2 volumes), Tübinger Perspektiven zur Pastoraltheologie und Religionspädagogik Volume 42, (Berlin: Lit, 2011). See also Ulrich Engel, 'Theorie-Praxis-Konstellationen. Zu einer Relecture der Pastoral/Theologie Marie-Dominique Chenus OP', *Freiburger Zeitschrift für Philosophie und Theologie*, 59 (2012): 531–536.

actions, of the right to and the necessity of subjectivity, of the positioning of the Church within society, of dialogue and openness (e.g. towards the separated churches, but also towards humanistic and Socialist thought), of self-criticism and new methods of pastoral work, of the importance of the laity and their having a say in things, of the renewal of theology, liturgy and ecclesiastical structures.[22]

The Dominicans in Le Saulchoir succeeded in making their mark through their theological position. Based on the work of their teacher Ambroise Gardeil OP (1859–1931), a 'study group'[23] of young theologians formed in the 1920s. This led to a reform of studies initiated by Gardeil.[24] This undertaking achieved a visible expression in the programmatic document published in 1937 under the title *Une école de théologie: Le Saulchoir*[25]—a little document, which was based on a speech held in Le Saulchoir one year before by Marie-Dominique Chenu. At that time he was Rector of the studium and Regent of Studies.

Chenu started from John 8:32: "The truth will set you free." In his programmatic lecture he drafted a 'collective self-portrait'[26] of Le Saulchoir. At the center of the school, Chenu recognised the spiritual freedom of Thomas Aquinas and the preacher brothers in the twentieth century:

---

22. Bunnenberg, 'In den Fängen des Hl. Offiziums', 20.
23. Müller, 'Was kann an der Theologie neu sein?', 91.
24. *Cf* Ambroise Gardeil, 'Les études dominicaines et les besoins présents in France. Rapport sur les Études présenté au Chapitre de la Province de France de 1901', in *Revue des Sciences Philosophiques et Théologiques*, 92/3 (2008): 433–459.
25. Marie-Dominique Chenu, *Une école de théologie: Le Saulchoir*. Avec les études de Giuseppe Alberigo, Étienne Fouilloux, Jean Ladrière et Jean-Pierre Jossua (Paris: Cerf, 1985). See also the very competent introduction to the German translation of 'Une école de théologie: Le Saulchoir' by Christian Bauer, 'Geschichte und Dogma. Genealogie der Verurteilung einer Schule der Theologie', M-Dominique Chenu, *Le Saulchoir. Eine Schule der Theologie*. Translated from French into German by Michael Lauble, edited by the Institut M-Dominique Chenu Berlin through Christian Bauer, Thomas Eggensperger and Ulrich Engel, Collection Chenu Volume 2 (Berlin: Morus, 2003), 9–50.
26. Étienne Fouilloux, 'Le Saulchoir en procès (1937–1942)', Marie-Dominique Chenu, *Une école de théologie: Le Saulchoir*. Avec les études de Giuseppe Alberigo, Étienne Fouilloux, Jean Ladrière et Jean-Pierre Jossua (Paris: Cerf, 1985), 39–59, here at 39.

It is also important for St. Thomas understanding to note that he lived in the time of St. Louis and Frederick II, at a time when the cities were fighting for their freedom, when the circulation of money changed the entire economy, when guilds witnessed the maturity of an entire class, when Notre Dame was built and the Rose Novel was written [. . .] St. Thomas was a daring and balanced master of this spiritual direction that created a new world. In these circumstances, he anchored himself in internal and external independence, in [. . .] spiritual freedom, which was a characteristic trait of his spirit, the foundations of which were [. . .] a passion for intervention, a sharp and at the same time cautious judgement in the paths of knowledge, and [. . .] a sincere contemplation of the truth that fanned the flames of inventiveness [. . .] These are the sources, foundations and certainties of our spiritual freedom in the 20th century, just as they were for St. Thomas in the 13th century.[27]

To preserve this freedom in the spirit of St Thomas he argued the three things are needed: 1) inventiveness, 2) scientific methodology, and 3) contemplation. For the Chenu, all three aspects form the 'spiritual milieu'[28] of the college and its teaching and learning community. In view of the Dominican motto of the order—'Veritas' (truth)—it was important for Chenu to think of *truth* and *freedom* together: "'The truth will make us free". Truth, that is freedom.'[29]

His listeners were thrilled. This reaction encouraged Chenu to publish the lecture. He revised, expanded and deepened his text. Chenu first published 'Une école de théologie: Le Saulchoir' in 1937 (128 pages). It recalls the history of the general study house of the Parisian Dominican Province from Saint-Jacques to Le Saulchoir (Chapter I). In Chapter II, he explains the spirit and methods which shape theology (Chapter III) and philosophy (Chapter IV) in Le Saulchoir. In Chapter V he makes concrete the theses using the example of medieval studies. A list of all publications published in Le Saulchoir up to 1936 concludes with this publication. With the permission of his provincial and with a print run of less than a thousand copies,

---

27. Marie-Dominique Chenu, 'Veritas liberabit vos. La Vérité vous rendra libres (Jn 8, 32)', in *Sources,* 16 (1990): 97–106, here at 100f.
28. Chenu, 'Veritas liberabit vos', 103.
29. Chenu, 'Veritas liberabit vos', 106.

the booklet was printed *pro manuscripto* by the Catholic publishing house Castermann in Tournai at the end of 1937. This means that the commemorative publication was only intended for internal use within the Order and therefore did not enter the public book trade.

The publication of *Une école de théologie: Le Saulchoir* coincided with two other important events in Chenu's term of office as rector. On June 29, 1937, the philosophical and theological faculties of the Salchoir were give recognition by Roman authorities. In the same year the university was able to return from its Belgian exile to Paris. Yves Congar remembers:

> We must have lived through this period to understand what hope it meant for us. With Fr. Chenu and in his retinue, we believed in theology and thought that it still had something to say to the people of today, provided that it was not content merely to rehash the formulas once found, but to seek an answer to the questions of the time.[30]

But soon dark clouds would be gathering over Le Saulchoir and its rector with a conflict between Rome and the Dominican at the Saulchoir.

In opposition to *Une école de théologie: Le Saulchoir* the magisterium soon opened proceedings into the Saulchoir and the book. In 1942, the Holy Office put the document on the Index of forbidden books. Johannes Bunnenberg writes that:

> An initial intervention from the magisterium took place already during the Second World War [. . .] Rome discovered modernistic echoes in it; a reawakening of modernistic tendencies seemed to the Roman authorities one of the main dangers facing the Church, along with Communism, because they feared an undermining of the faith. Chenu himself thought that the decisive point of the offence given was the application of the historical method to dogmatics, which reached its summit in the charge of relativism, which would undermine the unchanging truth of the faith. In February, 1938, Chenu was summoned to Rome and—to prove his

---

30. Yves Congar, 'Marie-Dominique Chenu', *Bilanz der Theologie im 20. Jahrhundert. Bahnbrechende Theologen*, edited by Herbert Vorgrimler and Robert Vander Gucht (Freiburg/Br: Herder, 1970), 99–122, here at 102.

orthodoxy—had to give his signature to ten theological theses without adding any commentary to them (no-one knows who drafted them).[31]

The ten theses, drafted in Latin,[32] read as follows:

1. Dogmatic formulas express a truth which is absolute and unchanging.
2. True and reliable statements, whether in philosophy or theology, are strong and not at all brittle.
3. Holy tradition does not create any new truths, but rather the deposit of revelation must be held on to in a decided way, as also to the sum total of divinely-revealed truths which was completed by the death of the last apostle.
4. Holy theology is not a kind of spirituality, which invents tools adapted to her religious experience, but rather she is a true science, praising God, won through zeal, whose foundations are the articles of faith and all revealed truths which theology subscribes to, through the divine gift of faith, at least imperfectly.
5. Different theological systems cannot be true at the same time, in so far as they contradict each other.
6. It redounds to the honour of the Church to hold the system of St Thomas for, as it were, orthodox in the highest degree, that is in particular agreement with the truths of the faith.
7. It is necessary to represent theological truths through Holy Scripture and tradition, but to illuminate their nature and inner reason through the principles and the teaching of St Thomas.
8. St Thomas was, in his person, even though he was a theologican in the proper sense of the term, also a philosopher; therefore, his philosophy, in its insights and truth, is not dependent on his theology, and it does not proclaim mere relative but absolute truths.
9. It is particularly necessary for the theologian, in his scientific method, to apply St Thomas' metaphysics and to follow exactly the rules of dialectics.
10. As for other recognised writers and doctors, strict moderation is to be maintainted in the way of speaking and writing about them, even when certain mistakes might have been found in their work.

---

31. Bunnenberg, 'In den Fängen des Hl. Offiziums', 20f.
32. Facsimile of the theses see: Chenu, *Une École de Théologie: Le Saulchoir*, 35.

A comparison makes clear how much these theses were contrary to Chenu's theological convictions. Recall the first thesis once again—concentrating particularly on the terms 'absolute' and 'unchanging'—and contrast this with a quotation from Chenu's congenial introduction to the work of St Thomas, where he refers to 'conditions' as 'means of access to that truth' and to the word 'historical':

The first thesis:

> 'Dogmatic formulas express a truth which is absolute and unchanging.'

Chenu's text:

> This whole work is based on the conviction that the works of a genius, in terms of their truth content and, therefore, in the understanding that we can gain from them, are closely linked with the society in which they have their roots, and can bear fruit over and beyond this society itself. There is no cleft between the spirit of inner truth and the conditions for confirming it, but rather, on the contrary, a constant interpenetration to the advantage of both of them. These conditions are, therefore, a real means of access to that truth, which does justice to the organic coming into being of that which is historical as well as the eternity of that which is true.[33]

Back to Le Saulchoir: putting Chenu's writing on the Index obviously was intended to affect not only the author himself but also other members of the Dominican research group,[34] above all Henri Marie Féret OP and Yves Congar OP, as well as Louis Charlier OP, a Belgian teaching in Louvain—but more than that: the House of Studies at Le Saulchoir was affected as a whole. Cardinal Emmanuel Suhard, the then Archbishop of Paris, consoled Chenu in a conversation with him as follows: 'Petite Père, do not be sad, in 20 years they will all be talking like you.'[35]

---

33. Marie-Dominique Chenu, *Das Werk des hl. Thomas von Aquin*. Translated from French into German by Otto M Pesch. Deutsche Thomas-Ausgabe. Ergänzungsband 2, Graz et al: Kerle ²1982, (18).

34. *Cf* the great scientific study of Michael Quisinsky, *Geschichtlicher Glaube in einer geschichtlichen Welt. Der Beitrag von M.-D. Chenu, Y. Congar und H.-M. Féret zum II. Vaticanum*, Dogma und Geschichte Volume 6 (Berlin: Lit, 2007).

35. *La liberté dans la foi*. Jacques Duquesne interroge le Père Chenu (Paris: Centurion 1975), 121.

Marie-Dominique Chenu OP (1895–1990)

Marie-Dominique Chenu deserves particular consideration, in as far as he was a central figure both of the *nouvelle théologie* as well as the worker priest's movement.[36] Outside France, his theological inheritance has been virtually forgotten; nevertheless, Chenu counts, in my view as one of the greatest of God's thinkers in the twentieth century. In the eventful biography of this 'theologian of the century',[37] the awakenings and the declines of around 100 years of Roman Catholic Church history mirror each other. Chenu represents unlike many others the 'Church spring'[38] in the time immediately after the Second World War in France, which was to come to fruition in terms of the worldwide Church in the Second Vatican Council (1962–1965).

Before it could come to this, however, in the period of thaw under Pope John XXIII, Chenu, as one of the leading figures in the 'Avant-garde of the Church',[39] had to survive a few spring frosts during the wintery latter part of the era of Pope Pius—his personal history of conflict with the Roman Magisterium coincided to a large extent with the pontificate of Pius XII.

---

36. After Jacques Loew OP began work in Marseille harbour in 1941 as the first worker priest in the strict sense, the number of worker priests increased quickly. From the year 1949 onwards, until the (provisional) abandonment of the experiment in 1954 as as result of the massive pressure from Rome, the almost 100 French worker priests met twice a year with, amongst others, Chenu, to exchange their experiences, which is why it is possible to talk about a movement of worker priests in this period. *Cf* on this U Engel, 'Bürgerliche Priester—proletarische Priester. Ein Lehrstück aus der Konfliktgeschichte zwischen Kirche und Arbeiterschaft', *Gott der Menschen. Wegmarken dominikanischer Theologie* (Ostfildern: Grünewald, 2010), 135–144; Ulrich Engel, '"Vital Opposition". Marie-Dominique Chenu O.P.—Fundamental Categories of His Theology Reflected in the Conflict Surrounding the French Worker-Priest Movement', *Angelicum*, 90 (2013): 961–976.
37. *Cf* Étienne Gilson: 'There is only one Fr. Chenu each century' (quoted according to Edward Schillebeeckx, 'In memory of Marie Dominique (Marcel) Chenu OP (7 January 1895—11 February 1990)', *I am a happy theologian*. Conversations with Francesco Strazzari, (New York: Crossroad, 1994), 89–92, here at 89.
38. Emmanuel Suhard, *Essor ou déclin de l'Église. Lettre pastorale. Carême de l'an de grâce 1947* (Paris: A Lahure, 1962), 174.
39. *Die Avantgarde der Kirche. Bahnbrecher des modernen Katholizismus in Frankreich. Texte und Dokumente 1942-1962*, edited by Jean-Marie Domenach und Robert Montvalon (Olten—Freiburg/Br: Walter, 1968).

As has already been mentioned, in 1942 *Une école de théologie: Le Saulchoir* was placed on the Index of forbidden books. Chenu, for whom this Roman sanction meant the immediate loss of his permission to teach, moved, after his replacement as rector of Le Saulchoir, to Paris, where he, according to the information provided by his fellow Dominican André Duval OP, lived intensively 'in the thirteenth'[40]: in the thirteenth century, the heyday of scholasticism, and in the 13th Arrondissement, a classical workers' district. Duval recalls it it in this way:

> And what does presence in the 13th Arondissement mean? It means (. . .) intelligent, passionate attention to all of that which represented 'Church in the state of mission' in P. Chenu's immediate and less immediate surroundings (by the way, this expression was coined by him). He was very close to the leading figures of the *Mission de France* and the *Mission de Paris*, he signed the Stockholm Appeal and got involved in various demonstrations of the peace movement. He spent his evenings with very different reflective groups: with members of the state council, with engineers, in working men's clubs, for which he felt spontaneous sympathy. 'Unshockable'—he was pleased to use this term about himself—he threw himself into the breach and thereby caused his best friends in the hierarchy a considerable amount of agitation.[41]

His moral and intellectial support for worker priests had been well-known for a long time. Already in the middle of the 1930s, Chenu had been interested in the matters concerning the workers' movement. After he had published his first pamphlet about the spirituality of work in 1940,[42] he kept returning to this subject—a examination of any bibliography of his works bears witnesses to this! Chenu soon also belonged to those professors whom one could regularly meet during the 'Semaines sociales de France'. In 1954, he published his theologi-

---

40. André Duval, 'M.-D. Chenu—Eine werkbiographische Skizze', M.-Dominique Chenu, *Leiblichkeit und Zeitlichkeit. Eine anthropologische Stellungnahme*, edited by the Institut M.-Dominique Chenu through Christian Bauer, Thomas Eggensperger and Ulrich Engel, Collection Chenu Volume 1), (Berlin: Morus, 2001), 61–75, here at 69.
41. Duval, 'M.-D. Chenu—Eine werkbiographische Skizze', 70.
42. Marie-Dominique Chenu, *Spiritualité du travail* (Paris: Temps Présent, 1940).

cal article about 'Le sacerdoce des prêtres-ouvriers'.[43] Several days later, there came the official ban on the experiment of worker priest movement. Because of Dominican based 'cleansing' that followed,[44] Chenu was transferred to Rouen in February of 1954, from where he nevertheless was able to return to Paris for one week every month, but full-time only in the year of the Council 1962.

Chenu always took up a clear position in the theological dispute between neo-scholasticism and *nouvelle théologie*. His 'thesis of dogma in the middle of history'[45] means (in contrast to the Roman position[46]) that dogmatic truth as such is eternal, but that the eternal salvation of humanity is being realised in history.[47]

As a Dominican who moved across the boundaries between faith and time, Church and world, dogma and pastoral work, Chenu was undertaking a 'theology of incarnation'.[48] It gained its creative originality in the unity of the tension of having an historical consciousness while being contemporary theoogy. And the tension in theology of the relationship between Church and world has lasted until to the present

---

43. Marie-Dominique Chenu, 'Le sacerdoce des prêtres-ouvriers', *L'évangile dans les temps. La parole de Dieu II*, (Paris: Cerf, 1964), 275–281. *Cf* Michael Quisinsky, 'Marie-Dominique Chenu, Le sacerdoce des prêtres-ouvriers (1954)', in *Wort und Antwort*, 54 (2013): 83–85.

44. Francois Leprieur, *Quand Rome condamne. Dominicains et prêtres-ouvriers* (Paris: Plon—Cerf, 1989), 77.

45. Hans-Joachim Sander, 'Die Zeichen der Zeit erforschen . . .' Die Bedeutung französischer Theologie für das Zweite Vatikanische Konzil, *Kirchliches Leben und Theologie in Frankreich. Dokumentation der Fachtagung in Kooperation mit der Arbeitsstelle für Jugendseelsorge zur Vorbereitung des Weltjugendtages in Paris 1997*, edited by Ute Franke-Hesse et al., KAJ Schriftenreihe Volume 5, (Odenthal-Altenberg: Katholische Akademie für Jugendfragen, 1997), 25–47, here at 35.

46. *Cf* as an example of this, the encyclical *Humani Generis*, which was aimed, amongst other things, at the 'nouvelle théologie', with which Pius XII. in 1950 turned those who 'want to reduce to a minimum the meaning of dogmas' (*Humani Generis* 14).

47. *Cf* Chenu, *Leiblichkeit und Zeitlichkeit*, 44.

48. *Cf* Claude Geffré, 'Théologie de l'incarnation et théologie des signes du temps chez le Père Chenu', *Marie-Dominique Chenu: Moyen-Âge et Modernité*, edited by Le Centre d'études du Saulchoir (Paris: Le Centre d'études du Saulchoir, 1997), 131–153; Ulrich Engel, 'Theologien der Inkarnation. Marie-Dominique Chenu OP (1895–1990) und Edward Schillebeeckx OP (1914–2009) im Spiegel neuerer Veröffentlichungen', in *Theologische Revue*, 109 (2013): 177–198.

times.[49] And, just like in the Middle Ages, the crucial question at the beginning of the 21st century is as follows: Pure and unblended theology versus a theology related to the world and is incarnatational?[50]

Opponents of the *Nouvelle Théologie*

The 'new' theological position of Chenu and his comrades-in-arms in Le Saulchoir was clear and unambiguous, and the opponents of the *nouvelle théologie* were also clear and unambiguous.

As regards France itself, we should mention a group of Dominicans from the Toulouse Province. They were located at the priory of Saint-Maximin. They formulated their position in 1951 under the title 'Sagesse' (wisdom), a document which was 'a pamphlet directed against "Une École de théologie: Le Saulchoir".[51]

More fundamental—because of graver consequence—was the opposition to the *nouvelle théologie* which gathered in Rome. This was to become the basis for all magisterial measures against the representatives of the new theology. Wolfgang W Müller writes:

> The Roman centre of criticism of the theological trend of Le Saulchoir had a name within the Order: the Angelicum, university of the Order, which regarded itself as the defender of 'pure' Thomism. The professorial body at the Angelicum was deeply rooted in the neo-scholastic tradition. The publication of the document 'Une école de théologie: Le Saulchoir' directly caused a stir of sensation in Rome, and, in addition, there was the publishing of the ecclesiological work 'Chrétiens désunies' by P. Yves Congars in 1938, which stirred up no less a sense of wrongdoing in Rome. The authorities of the Order demanded, through the superiors of Francia, an immediate withdrawal of Congar's book.[52]

---

49. *Cf* Ulrich Engel, 'A Church of and for the World. Marie-Dominique Chenu's Heritage as a Challenge to Contemporary Theology', in *Bulletin ET* 19/1 (2008): 141–146.

50. *Cf* in more detail on this: Christian Bauer, Thomas Eggensperger and Ulrich Engel, 'Geschichtsbewusstsein und Zeitgenossenschaft. Eine historisch-theologische Einführung in Band 1 der 'Collection Chenu', Chenu, *Leiblichkeit und Zeitlichkeit*, 7–20, here at 16–18.

51. Müller, 'Was kann an der Theologie neu sein?', 98 footnote 50. *Cf.* also on this see Jean-Pierre Jossua, 'Le Saulchoir revisité: 1937–1983', Chenu, *Une école de théologie: Le Saulchoir*, 83–90, especially 87f.

52. Müller, 'Was kann an der Theologie neu sein?', 98.

The following belonged to the most vehement of the critics:

- Michael Brown OP, at that time rector of the university of the Order in Rome and later Cardinal,
- Réginald Garrigou-Lagrange OP, member of the Toulouse Province and Professor at the Angelicum, who 'as a result of the magisterial measures against the new theological movement [was] sent as official visitator to France in order to hold a visitation of the non-observant priories'[53],
- and Mariano Cordovani OP, theologian of the Holy Office (the predecessor authority of the current Congregation for the Doctrine of the Faith).

In the end, the attacks carried out by Roman Dominicans against the representatives of the new theology à la Le Saulchoir (just as later against the Jesuits and their French House of studies Lyon-Fourvière) prepared the way for the official magisterial condemnation of the *nouvelle théologie*. This occurred in 1950 with the encyclical *Humani Generis*.

'The encyclical Humani Generis, published on 12 August 1950, by Pope Pius XII, undertook criticism of the new trends which were to be seen in theological science, but without naming names'. *One* quotation from the encyclical should make clear what was the direction of the attack of the magisterial text. Here, a theology which has as its point of departure human experience was rejected:

> There is also a certain historicism, which attributing value only to the events of man's life, overthrows the foundation of all truth and absolute law, both on the level of philosophical speculations and also that of Christian dogmas.[54]

Mgr Parente, who has already been mentioned at the beginning of this lecture, commented on the encyclical as follows:

> Apart from the polemical style, the remarks of the [Roman; *Ulrich Engel*] Dominicans [around Garrigou-Lagrange and his comrades-in-arms at the Angelicum; *Ulrich Engel*] were,

---

53. Müller, 'Was kann an der Theologie neu sein?', 99.
54. *Humani generis* 7.

for the most part, justified: [. . .] The encyclical recognises the form of dogmatic relativism with great exactness and condemns it.[55]

The Second Vatican Council (1962–1965)

In the course of the Second Vatican Council, it became clear that the victory of the Roman neo-scholastics over the representatives of the *nouvelle théologie* was, at the end of the day, only a Pyrrhic one. The devastating judgment which Garrigou-Lagrange and his comrades-in-arms had made, was corrected at the level of the whole Church. Looking at it from today's point of view, the history of theology assesses the *nouvelle théologie* positively as a forerunner of the Council. Looking back, Robert Aubert writes:

> If one attempted to put [the theological movement of the *nouvelle théologie*] in a nutshell [by means of a short afterword; *Ulrich Engel*], in the way that it portrayed itself in a somewhat overdone flaring-up around 1950, at the time when the encyclical Humani Generis marked the beginning of a declining line which determined the last years of the pontificate of Pius XII, then one could say that this theological movement, which was penetrated by a two-fold concern, namely that of returning to the sources and the other of opening up to the modern world, was situated exactly on the guideline showing where theology and the Church should always be.[56]

The opening up of the Church to the world was clearly to be seen in two Council texts: *Nuntius ad universos homines* (1962) and *Gaudium et spes* (1965). And, once again, Marie-Dominique Chenu participated in the writing of both of these texts. And yet Chenu's involvement at the Council was not at all a matter of course! For not until 1962—in the year in which the Second Vatican Council took up its

---

55. Pietro Parente, *La teologia*, Roma 1952, 68, quoted in the German translation by Müller, 'Was kann an der Theologie neu sein?', 103.

56. Quoted according to Rosino Gibellini, *Handbuch der Theologie im 20. Jahrhundert*. Translated from Italien to German by Peter F Ruelius (Regensburg: Pustet, 1995), 165.

work in Rome—was he able to return to Paris from his exile in Rouen.
And his road to Rome was also not the direct one, but rather he had
to take a 'diversion via Africa'.[57] Chenu was only able to get onto the
stage of the Council as the personal consultant of his pupil, Bishop
Claude Rolland of Antsirabe in Madagascar; he mainly worked there
behind the scenes—yet with great effect! 'The Message to Humanity' by the Council Fathers (*Nuntius ad universos homines*)[58] as well
as the 'Pastoral Constitution on the Church in the Modern World'
(*Gaudium et spes*)[59] show clear signs of his work.

The 'Message to Humanity', as the 'Declaration initiale' of the
Council, would not have come into being without Chenu's initiative.[60]
Nevertheless, Chenu's first draft of the text was considerably watered
down by the adaptation to the official 'clerical style'.[61] Chenu was
quoted as follows: 'You have dipped my little rascals in holy water'.[62]

And Chenu also participated directly in the coming into being
of the Pastoral Constitution, above all through his work in the sub-
committee 'Signs of the Times' which had been meeting since Sep-
tember, 1964.[63]

---

57. Marianne Heimbach-Steins, '"Erschütterung durch das Ereignis" (M-D Chenu).
    Die Entdeckung der Geschichte als Ort des Glaubens und der Theologie',
    *Visionen des Konzils. 30 Jahre Pastoralkonstitution 'Die Kirche in der Welt von
    heute'.* Schriften des Instituts für Christliche Sozialwissenschaften Volume 36
    (Münster: Lit 1997), 103–121, here at 107.

58. Second Vatican Council, 'The Message to Humanity (*Nuntius ad universos
    hominess*)', *Acta Apostolicae Sedis,* 54 (1962): 822–824.

59. Second Vatican Council, *Pastoral Constitution on the Church in the Modern
    World 'Gaudium et spes'.*

60. *Cf* André Duval, 'Le message au monde', *Vatican II commence . . . Appoches
    francophones,* edited by Étienne Fouilloux, Instrumenta theologica Volume 12
    (Leuven: Bibliotheek van de Faculteit der Godgeleerdheid, 1993), 105–118.

61. Marie-Dominique Chenu; quoted according to Heimbach-Steins, '"Erschütterung
    durch das Ereignis" (M.-D. Chenu)', 104.

62. Marie-Dominique Chenu; quoted according to Paulus Engelhardt, 'Neuaufbruch
    aus Tradition. Marie-Dominique Chenu', in *Wort und Antwort,* 31 (1990): 91–93,
    here at 93.

63. *Cf* Giovanni Turbanti, 'Il ruolo del P. D. Chenu nell'elaborazione della costitutione
    Gaudium et spes', *Marie-Dominique Chenu: Moyen-Âge et Modernité,* 173:
    'Tuttavia, tra i diversi filoni costutivi der documento e senza dubbio centrale
    quello ehe si richiama all'ispirazione teologica del p. Chenu, sottolineando il
    significato della storia e delle realtà terrestri e rivelando l'importanza die "segni
    die tempi" come luogo teologico dell'incamazione evangelica'.

Two short extracts from these texts are quoted here:

> 'Message to Humanity' (extract): In this assembly, under the guidance of the Holy Spirit, we wish to inquire how we ought to renew ourselves, so that we may be found increasingly faithful to the gospel of Christ. We shall take pains so as to present to the men of this age God's truth in its integrity and purity that they may understand it and gladly assent to it. (...) Coming together in unity from every nation under the sun, we carry in our hearts the hardships, the bodily and mental distress, the sorrows, longings, and hopes of all the peoples entrusted to us.[64]
>
> *Gaudium et spes* 4 (extract): To carry out such a task, the Church has always had the duty of scrutinising the signs of the times and of interpreting them in the light of the Gospel. Thus, in language intelligible to each generation, she can respond to the perennial questions which men ask about this present life and the life to come, and about the relationship of the one to the other.

These two Council texts, which were 'French' through and through, mark in a formal way (being the first and the last document decided upon by the Council), the beginning and conclusion of the Council. Apart from that, they also represent in a material way the new framework of Church practice which was set by the Council from the ground up.[65] Arising out of the direct dynamics of the Council itself, both stand as examples of this 'Concil à la dimension du monde' (Chenu). Both texts have as their subject, and, at the same time, achieve, a 'Copernican revolution'[66] of the Council to the world. Just as Nicolas Copernicus overcame the egocentricity of the Ptolemaic worldview on the threshold of modernity (the Earth as the centre of the universe), so the Council stepped over the shadow of its own ecclesiocentricity (the Church as the centre of the world), which had

---

64. Original in *Acta Apostolicae Sedis* 54 (1962), 822–824, here from Part II (Illuscescat facies Christi—May the Face of Christ Jesus Shine Out); and from Part IV (Caritas Christi urget nos—The Love of Christ impels us), quoted from Abbott, loc.cit.
65. *Cf* Heimbach-Steins, '"Erschütterung durch das Ereignis" (M.-D. Chenu)', 104f.
66. Marie-Dominique Chenu, 'Ein prophetisches Konzil', *Glaube im Prozeß. Christsein nach dem II. Vatikanum*, edited by Elmar Klinger and Karl Wittstadt, Festschrift Karl Rahner (Freiburg/Br: Herder, 1984), 16–21, here at 17.

been its own since the Constantinian revolution, on the threshold of post-modernity. From this point in time, what counted was, in the words of Chenu: 'No longer did the world revolve around the Church (. . .) but the Church revolved around the world.'[67]

By achieving this change of direction, the Church at last came out of its state of distancing itself from the world which characterised the 'Pius Epoch'. (The length of this epoch is usually thought of as lasting from the beginning of Pius IX's taking office in 1846 until the death of Pius XII in 1958.) The representatives of the *nouvelle théologie*, Chenu prominent among them, had prepared this 'jump forward'[68] of the Church into the world.

In the decades since the Council, Chenu vehemently stood up, through theological discussions, for the persistence of the conciliar awakening. He did this, for example, as one of the contributors to the international periodical *Concilium*. In this, he followed with particular sympathy the arising of liberation theology as a Latin American child of the Council; there are good grounds for counting Chenu, himself a pioneer of an earlier 'liberation theology in Europe',[69] as the spiritual father of Latin American liberation theology.

The post-conciliar developments in the ecclesiastical balance of power led to Chenu never being officially rehabilitated, let alone (like other representatives of the *nouvelle théolgie*) receiving a cardinal's hat as a recognition of his theological achievements.

---

67. Chenu, Ein prophetisches Konzil, 17.
68. Pope John XXIII, Gaudet mater ecclesia, Ludwig Kaufmann / Nikolaus Klein, *Johannes XXIII. Prophetie im Vermächtnis*, (Fribourg: Exodus, 1990), 116–150, here at 135.
69. *Cf* Ludwig Kaufmann, 'Ansätze einer Theologie der Befreiung in Europa? M.-D. Chenu (1895–1990), eine notwendige Erinnerung an französische Impulse', *Sozial- und Linkskatholizismus. Erinnerung—Orientierung—Befreiung*, edited by Heiner Ludwig and Wolfgang Schroeder (Frankfurt/M: Knecht 1990), 261–284; see also Ludwig Kaufmann, 'Gott im Herzen der Geschichte. M.-D. Chenu (1895–1990), eine notwendige Erinnerung an französische Impulse', Marie-Dominique Chenu, *Kirchliche Soziallehre im Wandel*. Translated from French into German by Kuno Füssel. Theologie aktuell, Volume 13 (Fribourg/Luzern: Exodus, 1991), 101–121.

Chenu's Theological Project*

Janette Gray, RSM

'Si vraiment l'homme connaît Dieu,
il le connaîtra humainement.'
['If man truly knew God, he would know him humanly']
Chenu, 'Position de la théologie' (1935) in *La Parole de Dieu I.*
La Foi dans intelligence (Paris: Cerf, 1964), 115–38, 119.

Introduction

Chenu's theology developed within theological limits set by two events: the endorsement of neo-scholastic Thomism by Pope Leo XIII as the universal theology for Latin Catholicism from 1879, and the proscription of any tendencies to theological 'modernism', from the pontificate of Pius X.[1] The intensely analytical scholasticism that resulted enshrined propositional content and a deductive method for theology. In this chapter Chenu's early theology is surveyed for its theological anthropological direction, especially the challenge his insistence on historicity posed to the neo-scholasticism of this period. Chenu labelled this 'modern scholasticism' to flag his belief that its true paternity was Enlightenment rationalism, not unbroken descent from medieval Thomism.[2]

---

* French translation into English by Patricia Kelly

1. In 1879 Leo XIII's encyclical *Aeterni Patris* called Catholic scholarship to reinstate the theological tradition of Aquinas, especially, but also Augustine and other Patristic sources. In Pius X's encyclical *Pascendi* (1907) neo-scholasticism was recruited to police theology. See Roger Aubert, 'The Modernist Crisis and the Integrist Reaction' in *The Church in a Secularised Society* (New York/ London: Paulist/ Darton, Longman and Todd, 1978), 198–203.

2. Chenu called this 'modern scholasticism' or, even more pejoratively, 'baroque scholasticism': 'Sous le patronage de Leibniz, cette qualification de

> Dans la technique quotidienne, c'est le formalisme logique
> qui triomphe au détriment de la curiosité, et à la «dispute»
> médiévale se sont substitués les «exercises scolastiques» qui
> n'en sont que la parodie dialectique.[3]
> [In the day-to-day technical work, it is logical formalism
> which has triumphed, at the cost of curiosity, and the medieval
> 'disputation' has been replaced by 'scholastic exercises' which
> are but a dialectical parody of it.]

This late scholasticism reduced theology to a philosophical apologetics which took on the rationalist style of the modernity it sought to
combat. Theology thus condemned itself to a solipsistic retreat to the
margins of the modern world.[4] Chenu initiated an innovative theo-

---

philosophia perennis nous invite à reconnaître, puis à situer—historiquement
et doctrinalement—certain idéal d'intelligibilité qui marqua la scolastique
moderne, et lui donne encore aujourd'hui le plus souvent sa tonalité. Cette
scolastique tendit à définir l'intelligible sous forme strictement rationnelle:
l'intelligible, c'est le concept qui s'analyse et qui s'attribue; le lien du réel, sa
structure intime est imaginée comme un lien de concepts' [Under Leibniz'
patronage, this qualification of *philosophia perennis* calls us to recognize and
then to situate historically and doctrinally a certain ideal of intelligibility which
marks modern scholasticism, and which still even today most often gives it
its tone. This scholasticism tended to define intelligibility in a strictly rational
way: what is intelligible is the concept which is analysed and attributed; the
link with the real, its intimate structure is imagined as a linking of concepts].
Une école de théologie: le Saulchoir, p. 83 [155]; cf also 'il apparaît bientôt que
des tranches entières de philosophie médiévale ont disparu, ou du moins ont
perdu leur densité spirituelle et systématique, dans la «scolastique» moderne, qui
revendique pourtant l'hériage de cette philosophie médiévale.' ['it soon seems
that entire sections of medieval philosophy had disappeared, or at least, had
lost their spiritual and systematic denseness, in modern "scholasticism", which
still claimed the inheritance of that medieval philosophy.'] 'Ratio superior et
inferior. Un cas de philosophie chrétienne', in *Revue des sciences philosophiques
et théologiques*, XXIX (1940): 84–89, 84.

3. *Une école*, 156. Chenu also termed this neo-scholasticism as the 'thomisme
    de séminaire'[seminary Thomism'] and 'thomisme régénéré par le kantisme'
    [Thomism regenerated by Kantism].
4. Chenu, 'Aux origines de la «science moderne»', in *Revue des sciences philosophiques
    et théologiques*, XXIX (1940): 206–217, 21; and 'Ratio superior et inferior. Un cas
    de philosophie chrétienne', in *Revue des sciences philosophiques et théologiques*,
    XXIX (1940): 84–89, 88; See the full elaboration of this view in Michael J.
    Buckley SJ, *At the Origins of Modern Atheism* (New Haven: Yale Unversity Press,
    1987). 341-2, 344-7, particularly 357: 'In failing to assert its own competence,

logical *rapprochement* with contemporary thought to circumscribe this marginalisation. He found authorisation for this in the example of Thomas Aquinas in the thirteenth century. Chenu's diachronic study of Thomas' full opus in its context showed the extent of 'modern scholastic' deviation from Thomas' theology. It revealed the scope of Thomas' engagement with his contemporary context and classical thought and contrasted Thomas' theology with the narrow systematisation digested into the manual theology of this time.[5]

After the 'modernist crisis' the historical status of theology and Revelation remained unresolved. Chenu's early publications betray his impatience with the atemporality and extrinsicism that passed for a 'superorthodoxie' ['hyper-orthodoxy'].[6] The perspective derived from his teaching of the history of doctrine gave him more critical historical purchase on doctrinal development. His uncommon theological openness to the challenges posed by contemporary philosophies disposed him to regard the 'Modernist crisis' as continuous with, not an aberration from, the celebrated theological achievements of the late nineteenth century.[7] These had awakened the Church to the urgent need for reform of theology through an engagement of faith with each historical situation.[8] Chenu wanted to restore the

---

in commissioning philosophy with its defense, religion shaped its own eventual negation.' and 358: 'Theology alienated its own nature by generating a philosophy that functioned as apologetics.'

5. The manual theology of Denzinger received further authorisation from the promotion of the digest of the 'Twenty-Four Theses' in 1914.

6. 'Le thomisme devenait pour eux une super-orthodoxie.' ['For them, Thomism became a hyper-orthodoxy.'] *Un théologien en liberté*, 32.

7. 'Les controverses et les incidents ultérieurs ne doivent ni dissimuler ni compromettre les fruits de cette très féconde activité, à laquelle présidait Léon XIII.' [Later controversies and incidents must neither cover up nor compromise the fruits of this most fertile activity, presided over by Leo XIII.] *Une école*, 35 [115]. Chenu provocatively included a 'Modernist' pantheon in *Une école*'s second chapter on 'Esprit et méthodes': Blondel, citation of a letter from George Tyrrel to Baron von Hügel, and a reference to Loisy.

8. 'Si, à tous ces étages, la controverse moderniste donna alors un caractère d'urgence à la «réforme de la théologie», comme on disait, les problèmes posés s'enracinaient en réalité beaucoup plus loin et engageaient toute l'histoire de la théologie moderne: *le statut des disciplines théologiques sur lequel nous vivons est celui des XVIe–XVIIe siècles, non celui des Sommes médiévales.*' ['If at every stage the modernist controversy gave an urgency to the "reform of theology", as they said, the problems raised had in reality taken root much further away and involved all

critical engagement of Catholic theology with contemporary life and thought by reclaiming the unity of the positive and speculative, mystical and doctrinal, and speculative and practical divisions of theology.[9] He advocated a theology that could integrate the experience of faith, situate doctrine within its human history, and draw out the human inclination to reason as constitutive of the dynamic of faith. After the negative allusions to such theology by Pope Pius XII to the Jesuit Congregation and later to the Dominican leadership in Rome such theology became known as 'nouvelle théologie', although those designated its proponents, Lubac, Chenu, Congar, and Daniélou, neither perceived themselves as nor acted as a movement.

His earliest theology focused on the rupture between speculative and 'mystical theology'. In Aquinas' teaching on contemplation, he uncovered faith presented as contemplation. For Chenu following Aquinas, faith is the affective experience of God's illuminating self-disclosure to each person that constitutes the desire for union with God and is grounded in human assent to the truths of Revelation. This is not a mindless affirmation of 'truths' or the confession of the 'deposit of faith'. Aquinas established the engagement of human intelligence in faith: that faith is unified in its formal and real qualities, and congruent with the process of all human reasoning. From this teaching, Chenu further derived the coherence of faith and theology in its historical contingency, as attested by the logic or grammar of the Incarnation. In this reading of Aquinas' teaching on faith, Chenu found elements for a theological anthropology more responsive to current epistemological concerns.

Faith as Contemplation

'Modernist' claims about theological development were not entirely constrained by the discipline of 'modern scholasticism'. From the early twentieth century there also emerged nascent spiritual, liturgical, missiological and ecumenical reform movements that would

---

the history of modern theology: *the status of theological disciplines in which we live is that of the 16ᵗʰ-18ᵗʰ centuries, not of the medieval Summae.*] *Une école,* 51–2 [129].

9. Chenu outlined the origins and outcomes of the separation of positive and speculative theology, the extremes of 'historicisme et theologisme', in his later summary of his theology: *La théologie est-elle une science?* (Paris: Athème Fayard, 1957), 110–112.

slowly move the Church towards Vatican II. These movements subverted the spiritual and critical deficiencies of the official neo-scholastic theology. They represent the dynamic currents hidden in Catholic theology in the late nineteenth and early twentieth centuries. The 'Modernist crisis' and Blondel's turn to experience and historical consciousness had inflicted an irreversible change of direction in theology. No longer was the Kantian turn to experience resistible by the philosophical exclusivity of neo-scholasticism. It had insinuated itself into Church life and then into theology through the experiential modes and particularity of these reform movements. The epistemological need to engage with the reality of the spiritual life of Christians then raised unavoidable problems from within for the neo-scholastic metaphysics. Chenu's theology was formed within two different schools of this theological revival. He learnt what he termed 'l'équilibre spirituel' ['spiritual equilibrium'] at Le Saulchoir led by Ambroise Gardeil, a founding proponent of the return to textual criticism. At the Angelicum, he studied at the heart of the Roman spiritual revival with Réginald Garrigou-Lagrange. Theology at Le Saulchoir was already shaped by the Tübingen School's ecclesiology and a concern for a revived theology of grace. Chenu's 1920 doctoral thesis on contemplation in Aquinas reveals the substantial influence of Tübingen's Möhler and his mystical ecclesiology.[10] Another source was the Jesuit Pierre Rousselot who recovered the intellectual component of contemplation in Aquinas.[11] Chenu contributed his critical

---

10. Extracts from Chenu's thesis are cited in CG Conticello's study, '*De Contemplatione* (Angelicum 1920) La thèse inédite de doctorat du P M-D Chenu', in *Revue des sciences philosophiques et théologiques*, 75/3 (1991): 363–422.

11. Chenu was influenced by Gardeil's debate with Rousselot's position on the intrinsically divine value of the human intellect. Chenu approved of Rousselot's teaching that the grace of faith included a divine illumination, which made it possible to see the natural grounds for making the act of faith. Chenu quoted Rousselot in his thesis, cited in Conticello, '*De Contemplatione*', 401: 'Le point capital est que, pour S. Thomas, la faculté qui nous fait capables de cette action transcendante (vision, contemplation de Dieu) est identiquement celle qui, selon une autre mode d'agir, forme nos concepts et combine nos deductions . . .' ['The point is that for St Thomas the faculty which makes us capable of this transcendent action (vision, contemplation of God) is identical to that faculty which, in another mode of action, forms our ideas and devises our deductions . . .'] Pierre Rousselot SJ, *L'intellectualisme de saint Thomas* (Paris: Alcan, 1908), 38–40.

ressourcement of the complete Aquinas corpus to this revival, which informed his early methodological studies.[12]

Chenu's thesis on contemplation launched not only this *ressourcement* of Aquinas' theological method and development but several recurring subjects in his theology: the meaning of faith, doctrinal development, reconciliation of the ruptured ascetic and mystical, positive and speculative theology, and the unity of theological understanding and theological contemplation of God. In these are evidenced the characteristic anthropological direction of his later theology. His scepticism about neo-scholastic metaphysics came through his preference for historical locating Thomas' teaching. Chenu's optimistic vision of humanity and the world, countering Augustinian dualism and contempt for the world also appeared in the thesis and his quest for a theological equilibrium between reality and mystery, nature and grace, contemplation and action were introduced.

Chenu took as his starting point the current theological debate about the nature and distinction of mystical states and the scope of their occurrence: whether mystical experience and contemplation were restricted to a spiritual elite.[13] For Thomas, mystical contemplation is integral to the Christian life as the normal fruit and end of baptismal grace. In contemplation, the gifts of the Holy Spirit perfect humanity by drawing it to union with God. Evident in Thomas' teaching about this question is his use of Pseudo-Dionysius to reject the aristocratic restriction of mystical experience, invoking his understanding that contemplation consists of a knowledge-experience of God, through the *mystagogy* of divine action which engages the con-

---

12. 'Ce n'est donc pas par manie d'antiquaire que j'ai recherché et cité quelques textes de théologiens ou philosophes assez obscurs du 13e siècle; mais parce qu'il est indispensable pour atteindre la pensée de S. Thomas de la remettre dans le milieu où elle est née, où elle s'est développée, selon telle ou telle réaction, sous telle influence' ['Thus it is not because of an antiquary's obsession that I have researched and quoted texts from rather obscure thirteenth-century theologians or philosophers; rather, that it this is indispensable for reaching St Thomas' thought and putting it back in the environment in which it was born and developed, following such and such a reaction or influence'], in *De Contemplatione*, 5–6, in Conticello, 386.

13. The key antagonists were A. Poulain SJ, who advocated a pure mysticism, of an extraordinary and miraculous nature restricted to a few blessed souls, and A. Saudreau who held the more ancient concept of spirituality/mysticism as accessible to all, ie 'infused contemplation'. Conticello, p. 371.

naturality of the human's creatureliness with the Creator's initiative in creation.[14] Chenu's examination of Aquinas' sources, in relation to this debate, disclosed the impact of Greek Patristic theology and neoplatonic thought on Aquinas, particularly his debt to Dionysius as much as to Augustine. This identification of Aquinas' dependence on Augustine's' psychological theology and Dionysius' spiritual theology rejected the prevalent reduction of the *Summa theologiae* to a theological Aristotle and provided the key to reclaiming the medieval theological synthesis: a revised theology of faith. The references to Dionysius in this thesis are also significant as the earliest evidence of Chenu's zeal to propagate the importance of the theology of the East for Latin theology, not merely to balance a lop-sided Christian theology, but to augment deficient interpretations in the Latin tradition.[15] Chenu also employed this teaching on contemplation to overturn the 'aristocratique' distinction of mystical contemplation from the commonplace *ascesis*. Such understanding later informed Chenu's conviction about the Christian vocation of the laity and his involvement in lay formation and other practical anticipations of the 'universal call to holiness' in Vatican II's *Lumen Gentium*.

Even more significant for Chenu's theology was the location of contemplation as integral to the Christian life of faith. The relationship between contemplation and faith then drew Chenu's examination. As

---

14. Pseudo-Dionysius, *Divine Names*, II, 9 (*PG* 3, 648B), cited in Conticello, 414–5. The Dominican school, promoters of the unity of the spiritual life, defended the argument for a broad mysticism based in a theology of the gifts of the Holy Spirit, as elaborated by Gardeil and Garrigou-Lagrange. Conticello, 373 n 38.

15. A later example is found in 'Position de la théologie' (1935), 127: 'Le théologien latin réduira le symbole à une *signe* dont l'intelligibilité va être définissable et l'expression juridiquement classée; mais l'oriental conservera au sacrement son nom de *mystère*, et Denys voit dans le culte un milieu d'opération déifiante.' ['The Latin theologian reduces the symbol to a *sign* whose intelligibility will be definable, and whose expression can be classified legally, while the Eastern theologian maintains the term *mystery* for the sacrament, and Denys sees an environment of deifying operations in worship.'] Chenu did not oppose Latin and Greek theologies, a simplification common in twentieth century theology. Michel René Barnes discredits this false dichotomy in 'Augustine in Contemporary Trinitarian Theology', in *Theological Studies*, 56 (1995): 237–250, 237–242. Chenu's promotion of Eastern theology and his mediation for the Eastern bishops at the Second Vatican Council was his most direct and effective contribution. See *Notes quotidiennes au Concile: Journal de Vatican II 1962–1963* (Paris: Les Éditions du Cerf, 1995), 107–110, 123, 130–132.

he would later describe this: 'La foi est vraiment alors l'amorce de la vision béatifique, la prélibation de la contemplation future.' ['Thus faith really is the beginning of the beatific vision, the foretaste of future contemplation.'][16] Chenu was influenced by Gardeil's recovery of Thomas' concept of the supernatural inner illumination of faith (*synderesis*). Through this light the Holy Spirit who reveals the truths of Revelation also integrates faith as intrinsic to human experience.[17] This understanding of the supernatural character of faith overturned the need for an extrinsic definition of faith: in order to preserve the divine continuity between Revelation, faith, and theology, faith was located outside any possible human contamination. Affirming faith's supernatural integrity, then Chenu outlined the human reality in which faith is grounded. He asserted that the believer's assimilation to God, who as the object sought and known, is the sole goal and source of all human understanding. This included the activity of both the intuitive and affective properties of contemplation as much as the volitional character of assent.[18] Here Chenu demonstrated his early scepticism about the reductive effect on the doctrine of faith of the deductive metaphysics of modern scholasticism, which marginalised doctrine from the life experience of faith, and segmented the unity

---

16. A later example is found in 'Position de la théologie' (1935), 127: 'Le théologien latin réduira le symbole à une *signe* dont l'intelligibilité va être définissable et l'expression juridiquement classée; mais l'oriental conservera au sacrement son nom de *mystère*, et Denys voit dans le culte un milieu d'opération déifiante.' Chenu did not oppose Latin and Greek theologies, a simplification common in twentieth century theology. Michel René Barnes discredits this false dichotomy in 'Augustine in Contemporary Trinitarian Theology', in *Theological Studies*, 56 (1995): 237–250, 237–242. Chenu's promotion of Eastern theology and his mediation for the Eastern bishops at the Second Vatican Council was his most direct and effective contribution. See *Notes quotidiennes au Concile: Journal de Vatican II 1962–1963* (Paris: Les Éditions du Cerf, 1995), 107–110, 123, 130–132. Chenu, *La théologie est-elle une science?*, 31.

17. Gardeil clarified the formal object of faith and with Garrigou-Lagrange restored the emphasis on faith's supernatural character. Gardeil's recovery of Aquinas' teaching on the illumination of faith, *lumen fidei*, the inward light of the Holy Spirit bridging Revelation and the believer in ways that human understanding can perceive, was particularly influential. Roger Aubert, *Le problème de l'acte de foi*, 587; Schoof, *Breakthrough*, 189–190.

18. Conticello, 386–88. Conticello notes that Chenu referred frequently to Garrigou Lagrange in his thesis, while Gardeil is seldom cited although his influence pervades the whole work, *cf* 377, and n 44.

of theology into discrete spiritual, doctrinal or pastoral categories. For Chenu, continuity with the patristic and medieval understanding of theology required instead a dynamic nexus between the spiritual, doctrinal and pastoral aspects of theology. Chenu's later research on the epistemological and psychological structure of the act of faith was anticipated in this analysis of the formal elements in the genesis of the believing act, the assent to attested truths (*auditus fidei*), and the interior call of God. The dynamic of the understanding of the faith (*fides quaerens intel- lectum*) is not a simple conceptual knowing, but a progressive assimilation to the first Truth through the ways of human understanding.[19] For Chenu there is no *auditus fidei* without an *intellectus fidei*, and the object of faith is neither of these but God.

Central to Chenu's study of Thomas' understanding of contemplation was a concern for theological realism. Rejecting the Augustinian and neo-scholastic dichotomy between human religious perception and other human conceptualisation, Chenu embraced St Albert the Great's and St Thomas' teaching on the unity of human cognition: the same intellectual faculty that generates all other acts of cognition, for acquiring any other knowledge, is that engaged in contemplation and any graced vision of God.[20] Such an understanding was underpinned by a Dominican optimism about humanity and the world, that homogeneous view of the relationship of nature and grace so characteristic of Thomas' anthropology. Chenu emphasised that, for Aquinas the gap between humanity and God is not bridged by means of the negation of human freedom, nor by a Buddhist-like renunciation of will, but in the human act of recollection. Such recollection is the essential yet freely chosen unifying of all the creature's being and activity with God.[21] This demonstrated for Chenu the homogene-

---

19. Conticello, 408.
20. Chenu: 'C'est là le point de divergence, non seulement de deux théories *peri psychés*, mais de deux mentalités, de deux spiritualités, de deux mystiques.' ['This is the point of divergence not only of two theories *peri psychés*, but also of two mind-sets, two spiritualities, and two mysticisms.'] *De Contemplatione*, 40, cited in Conticello, 400–401.
21. 'La simplicité intellectuelle du contemplatif ne s'opère pas par en bas dans un état negatif, à la façon d'un bouddhiste, mais par en haut: elle est non simplification par appauvrissement—celle des hallucinés—mais par enrichissement. ['The contemplative's intellectual simplicity does not operate from below in a negative state, like that of a Buddhist, but from on high: it is not a simplification through impoverishment—as with hallucinations—but through enrichment.'] *Totus*

ity or continuity between human knowledge of God and the data of
God's Revelation, in contrast to the negative view of the human condition prevalent in seventeenth and eighteenth century spiritualities,
still influential on twentieth century Catholic life. Consistent with his
Dominican background, the horizon of Chenu's thesis is theocentric:
God is supremely intelligible. It was thus not specifically Christocen-
tric, which was more characteristic of Augustinian, Franciscan and
Jesuit spiritualities.[22] This was in contrast to his emphasis on the 'loi
de l'Incarnation' ['law of the incarnation'] in his theology after 1937.
There is an early orientation towards anthropological theology in the
centrality afforded by Chenu to the human understanding of faith in
Aquinas' theology of contemplation.

Chenu found in contemporary studies on the psychology of
the spiritual life support for the psychological realism of the unity
of theology, of contemplation and faith. He referred particularly to
Bergson's vitalist phenomenology and Maréchal's transcendental
epistemology of the dynamism of human spirit.[23] These psychological
arguments did not meet with Garrigou-Lagrange's approval. Despite
recovering the spirituality of St John of the Cross and reinstating the
academic study of spiritual theology, Garrigou-Lagrange maintained
its separation from dogmatic theology and regarded such interdisciplinary scope as insufficiently focused on Thomas.[24] In contrast, these

---

*labor meditationis, cogitationis, reflexionis, etc, quo homo ascendit et pervenit
ad simplicem intuitum contemplationis, fundatur psychologice in hac doctrina S.
Thomae', De Contemplatione*, 19–20, in Conticello, 396.

22. *De Contemplatione*, 8–9, in Conticello, 384, n 51; 387 n 55.
23. Conticello, pp. 379–80. The influence of Maréchal's transcendental synthesis
    on Chenu (initially in 'La mystique chrétienne', in *Revue de philosophie*, 2
    (1912): 445–446) is not sustained, despite André Hayen SJ's detection of an
    unacknowledged echo in *La théologie comme science au XIIIe siècle*. 'La théologie
    comme science aux XIIe, XIIIe et XXe siècles', in *Nouvelle Revue Théologique*, 79
    (1957): 1009–1028, 1011–1012, notes 37, 38.) The reference cited demonstrates
    moreChenu's dependence on Maréchal for his valuing the Dionysian theology of
    contemplation.
24. 'Garrigou-Lagrange lui-même, qui a patronné généreusement ma thèse, était un
    peu effarouché par l'introduction de l'analyse psychologique dans un phénomène
    qui, de soi, est «surnaturel». Heureusement, mon analyse théologique lui plaisait
    beaucoup.' ['Garrigou-Lagrange himself, who generously supervised my thesis,
    was somewhat alarmed by the introduction of psychological analysis into
    a phenomenon which is in itself "supernatural". Fortunately my theological
    analysis delighted him.'] Chenu, *Un théologien en liberté*, 38.

extra-scholastic sources demonstrated for Chenu the psychological realism of the unity of faith and contemplation.[25] Chenu's insistence on the coherence of faith and contemplation repaired the dismemberment of the mystical from doctrinal theology:

> Il faut manifester la valeur contemplative, «mystique», de l'intelligence (*intellectus ut intellectus*), et maintenir sa prépondérance jusque dans les mystérieuses profondeurs de l'union mystique, où, là comme partout ailleurs, elle est puissance d'ordre lumière. Point donc d'opposition fausse et vaine . . . Le mysticisme, a-t-on dit, est pour Saint Thomas intellectualisme intégral.[26]

> [We must demonstrate the contemplative, 'mystical' value of understanding (*intellectus ut intellectus*) and maintain its ascendency even within the mysterious depths of the mystical union, where, there as elsewhere, it is a power of the order of light. There is thus no false and vain opposition. . . . It has been said that for St Thomas, mysticism is fully intellectualism.]

In his thesis Chenu emphasised the unity of spiritual and speculative theology in Thomas and refuted a common tendency to oppose Thomas' intellectualism with the mysticism of Anselm, Bonaventure and Scotus:[27] Chenu thus contributed to the spiritual renewal recog-

---

25. 'En tout cas, il est représentatif qui imprégnait, depuis un siècle, les lettres, les arts, la morale, le droit . . . Non plus foi en la Parole, dont l'appétit se nourrit d'intelligence contemplative et rationnelle, *fides quaerens intellectum*, mais combinat hétérogène d'autorité et de raison: après une enquête dite positive, la théologie s'organise en «science des conclusions»—c'est l'expression ingénument employée—, qu'on tire, selon les lois de la logique, d'un dossier extérieur.' ['In any case it is representative of something which, for a century, has permeated literature, arts, morality, law . . . it is no longer faith in the Word, for which the appetite is nourished by rational and contemplative understanding, *fides quaerens intellectum*, but combines a heterogeneity of authority and reason. Following a so-called positive enquiry, theology is organised as a "science of conclusions"—this is the clever expression which is used—which is drawn, according to the laws of logic, from an external folder.'] Chenu, 'La littérature comme "lieu" de la théologie', in *Revue des sciences philosophiques et théologiques*, LIII (1969): 70–80, 73.

26. *De contemplatione*, 3 (Chenu's brief insertion in French to the introduction). *Cf* also page 60, Chenu criticises: 'pseudo-mystici, qui despiciunt cognitionem tanquam impedimentum et obstaculum amoris'.

27. *De contemplatione*, 3, in Conticello, 383.

nising the need to restore the coincidence of *speculatio* and *contemplatio*, that contemplation in faith is constitutive of all theology.[28]

His historical situating of Thomas with 'minor' Franciscan spiritual writings in the thesis, to ascertain the genealogy of Thomas' teaching on contemplation, drew portentous warning from his teacher, Garrigou-Lagrange.[29] Chenu later identified this resistance to historical perspective on theology as the point of division between him and Garrigou-Lagrange. Chenu's trawling of the Western spiritual tradition yielded a more nuanced differentiation of Thomas' theology, and of other Dominican theologians, from the dualist spirituality of the neo-Augustinians. This in turn revealed to him the extent of the deviation of the Augustinians from Augustine's thought.[30] Making its debut in these distinctions is Chenu's trademark abhorrence of any psychological dualism or spiritual rejection of the world. More than merely mapping the diversity in scholastic positions, he was detecting a hitherto ignored inclusiveness as integral to Aquinas' theology. This provided an authoritative corrective to the narrow selection and prejudice of 'modern scholasticism's' method and sources. Chenu found modelled in Thomas' synthesis and elucidation of conflicting sources an aversion to exclusive concentration on one theological author or system.

Chenu's doctoral study of contemplation in Aquinas, with its methodological innovation and psychological curiosity evidences his early concern with the failure of 'modern scholasticism' to preserve the unity of human cognition. Its inability to acknowledge the historical context of Thomas' theology and anthropological concerns boosted the persistence of the dichotomisation of asceticism and mysticism, spirituality and theology, faith and reason, experience of historical event and doctrine. The historian Boureau noted, that the historical incarnation of theological thought which Chenu established in his doctoral thesis, remained his constant conviction

---

28. Conticello, 391.
29. Conticello, 379–80. Chenu's later explanation of this was that Garrigou-Lagrange was 'a complete stranger to history' and its significance: *Un théologien en liberté*, 38.
30. The Franciscans cited were John Rupellensis, J Peckham and St Bonaventure. His Dominican authorities were Master Eckhardt, Henry Suso, Johannes Tauler. Other later 'spirituels' included Ruysbroeck, Angelo Foligno, Jeanne de Chantal, Francis de Sales, Teresa of Avila and John of the Cross. Pseudo-Dionysis is the most frequently cited source.

from this time in Rome to his activism with workers in 1950's Paris. This tight connection between the intellectual and spiritual in human being is the core of all his theology.[31] Separation of this connection, so marked in the extrinsicism of 'modern scholasticism', is at the dreadful cost of denying the divine activity in Creation and Incarnation. Chenu's theological project began as a rejection of these oppositions. In demonstrating faith as contemplation in Aquinas, Chenu began his lifelong commitment to the unity of theology, human inquiry and contemplation of God.

Faith in understanding

Chenu recognised that the discounting of human experience by 'modern scholasticism' restricted the role of reason in the doctrinal assent of faith.[32] This quarantined neo-scholastic theology in an unchecked extrinsicism. Only a renewed understanding of the intellectual dimension of faith could relieve this theological stand-off to reveal the anthropological condition of faith and reason. For Chenu, this underscored the contemporary need to continue the medieval synthesis of reason and restore human understanding as integral to faith: *la Foi dans intelligence*.[33]

In three seminal studies on *Summa Theologiae* IIa IIae, q. 1, a. 2, Chenu recovered a neglected part of Thomas' teaching regarding the intellectual quality of faith. The object of faith is God, a reality, not those propositions compounded into a deposit or body of dogma.[34]

---

31. Alain Boureau, 'Le Père Chenu médiéviste: historicité, contexte et tradition', *Revue des sciences philosophiques et theologiques,* 81 (1997): 407–414, 410–11.
32. 'Contribution à l'histoire du traité de la foi. Commentaire historique de IIa IIae, q. I, a. 2' (1923) in *La Parole de Dieu I. La Foi dans intelligence* (Paris: Cerf, 1964), 31–50, 48. Louis Dupré commented on 'the clearcut separation between spiritual doctrine and School theology': 'This isolation, in the end fatal to both, freed spiritual life from the burden of an incompatible theology and rendered it more congenial to the modern age. Theology's severance from the religious experience, once an integral part of *contemplatio*, had marginalized it with respect to culture as well as to piety.' *Passage to Modernity* (New Haven: Yale University Press, 1993), 222.
33. Hence Chenu chose this emblematic expression as the title for his first collection of writings: *La Parole de Dieu I: La Foi dans intelligence*.
34. 'Ergo objectum fidei non est enuntiabile, sed res.'*Summa Theologiae* IIa IIae, q. 1, a. 2, ad. 2.

The human subject receives this Revelation in a complex of propositions about the object of faith, because of the ontological differ-
ence between God and the creature, and the limitations of human
understanding.[35] Chenu emphasised the importance of this formal
distinction, that the object known to us from Revelation is necessarily
complex, while the object itself, God, remains simple.

> La connaissance de foi est une connaissance humaine et
> terrestre, complexe, et donc essentiellement progressive; la
> vision seule est simple et immobile, «*per modum simplicis
> intelligentiae*».[36]
> [The knowledge of faith is a human, earthly, complex
> knowledge, and therefore is of its essence progressive; the
> vision alone is simple, unmoving, "*per modum simplices
> intelligentiae*".]

Thomas assigned to human understanding, not to human volition,
the reception of the self-disclosure of God, thereby categorically
affirming the human character of the act of faith.[37]

Chenu found that the key to interpreting Thomas' teaching on
faith was the reply to article 2: what is knowable about the object
of faith comes by the same means of knowing as all other human
knowledge, *cognita sunt in cognoscente secundum modum cognoscentis*.[38] Integral to faith and to human knowledge of God is the same act
of judgement, the weighing-up and clarification of what is revealed,
and then assent to a complex of propositions. Such coming to judgement is definitive of human understanding not merely accidental to
it. This is the action of the governing virtue of prudence.

> La prudence ne s'ajoute pas de l'extérieur à la raison et à la
> volonté, comme un devoir s'impose à la liberté pour la
> contraindre: c'est la raison même, rendue parfaite, dans son
> jugement et dans ses choix. Elle intériorise, elle personnalise

---

35. 'Contribution à l'histoire du traité de la foi', 48.
36. *ST* IIaIIae, q.1, a.2, ad. 3. Chenu, 'La raison psychologique du développement du
    dogme d'après Saint Thomas' (1924) in *La Parole de Dieu I*, 52–58, 57.
37. 'Contribution à l'histoire du traité de la foi', 49.
38. *ST* IIa IIae, q. I, a. 2, *responsio*. 'Contribution à l'histoire du traité de la foi', 48–49;
    'La raison psychologique', 53. Chenu repeatedly uses this text also to justify the
    use of sociological method in theological reflection.

la loi, au point que là seulement, dans ma conscience, je puis parler décidément d'obligation.[39]
[Prudence is not added from the outside to reason and will, as a duty is imposed on freedom to constrain it: it is reason itself, made perfect in its judgement and its choices. It interiorises and personalises the law, to the extent that only there, in my conscience, can I truly speak about obligation.]

Dogmatic truth presents itself structurally and dynamically as an affirmation of human understanding, with all the complexity involved in all other human knowledge and judgement.

la lumière de foi ne modifiera pas notre mécanisme conceptual, nos procédés d'élaboration, de penetration . . . sans nuire à l'unité et à l'immutabilité de la foi ni non plus à sa «réalité».[40]
[the light of faith will not change our conceptual mechanism, our processes of elaboration and penetration . . . without harming the unity and immutability of faith nor its 'reality'.]

Chenu found in this reply Thomas' heuristic principle. Any descriptions of faith which compromise the unity of human spirit by their heterogenous separation of faith from other human knowing are exposed as deficient through this principle.

Resituating faith in its human condition required an account of the development of doctrine. For Chenu the problem of the immutability of faith and the development of doctrine is not solved by opposing a timeless concept of faith with a judgement determined in time, because 'la foi est de la terre' ['faith is earthly'], faith is ever conditioned by human ways of knowing and history:

saint Thomas admet désormais que la détermination temporelle est partie essentielle de l'acte de foi, comme d'ailleurs de toute proposition: nous devons croire que «le Christ est né», au passé. Il va donc falloir reconnaître entièrement les «variations» de la foi.[41]
[St Thomas now allows that temporal determination is an essential part of the act of faith, as it is, moreover, of any proposition: we must believe that 'Christ was born', in the

---

39. *St Thomas d'Aquin et la théologie*, 145.
40. 'La raison psychologique', 53–4.
41. 'Contribution à l'histoire', 47.

past. It will therefore be necessary to fully acknowledge the
'variations' of faith.]

He emphasised also the psychological reality of the subjective cognition involved in dogmatic formulation.[42]

> Complexité et «pluralité» sont notes essentielles de la
> connaissance de foi parce qu'elle sont notes essentielles de la
> connaissance humaine. Ainsi le dogme a une histoire parce
> qu'il est sujet au progrès (homogène et infaillible de par
> l'assistance de l'Ésprit-Saint) de l'énoncé humain.[43]
> [Complexity and 'plurality' are essential traits of the knowledge
> of faith because they are essential traits of human knowledge.
> Thus dogma has a history because it is subject to the progress
> of human pronouncements (albeit homogenous and infallible
> thanks to the aid of the Holy Spirit).]

Thomas' realism led him to a categorical affirmation of the temporal
character of the human act of faith. From this Chenu drew both the
authority and method to approach the problem of the development of
doctrine. Chenu recovered Aquinas' method of dialectic, and ability
to judge between different readings across the tradition, all of which
had escaped other modern Thomist commentators.

> La genèse de cette méthodologie, ses préparations, ses
> réactions, les résistances qu'elle rencontra, rendaient
> témoignage à ce grand oeuvre de saint Thomas, dont les
> textes, ainsi lus dans leur milieu natif, prenaient une vigueur
> historique, à l'appui d'une interprétation interne solidement
> tenue depuis sept siècles.
> [The genesis of this methodology, along with the preparation,
> reactions, and resistance it would encounter, bore witness
> to that great work of St Thomas whose texts, when read in

---

42. Contra Guillaume d'Auxerre's *Summa aurea*, lib. III, tr. 3, cap. I, q. 5: 'la théorie de
    l'*explicatio implicatorum*, formule encore un peu simpliste chez lui' ['the theory of
    the *explicatio implicatorum*, a formula which he still uses rather simplistically']:
    'La raison psychologique du développement du dogme d'après Saint Thomas'
    (1924) in *La Parole de Dieu I. La Foi dans intelligence* (Paris: Cerf, 1964), pp.
    51–58, 52. Chenu noted that this theory applied to the progress of Revelation not
    the development of dogma, 53, n 4.
43. 'La raison psychologique du développement', 54.

their native environment, took on a historical force, with the support of an internal interpretation which was solidly held for seven centuries.][44]

Thomas saw analogy between the development of other human knowledge and the way that dogma evolves and is elaborated. Chenu's *ressourcement* of Thomas thereby undermined the strategy of separation foundational to 'modern-scholasticism'.

Chenu's interest in restoring the role of reason in theology drew him to probe Thomas' text for its more nuanced anthropological observations about faith and theology. Thomas had provided such an example in his synthesis of the long-received Augustinian psychology with the new 'science' of Aristotle's epistemology.[45] In what Chenu described as a profound theological echo of St Augustine's famous cry, Thomas asserted that the restlessness of human inquiry is of the nature of faith and is fuelled by its origin and end in the natural human desire to see and know God.[46] Hence desire for union with God, for life eternal, constitutes all action and knowing, and is an analogue of reason within human inquiry. The human restlessness to understand is integral to faith. Thomas' solution was that fidelity to God is not grounded in the passivity of certitude, nor even of willing obedience, but in 'l'inquiétude' ['the anxiety'] that drives all human understanding.

> La densité de ce texte du *De Veritate* dépasse en puissance d'émotion et en valeur religieuse les plus pascaliennes pensées; il ne trouvera réplique que dans les descriptions anxieuses du mystique avançant dans les «ténèbres» de la foi. Mais aux yeux du théologien, ce par quoi il vaut, c'est par la qualification donnée à cette inquiétude, plus encore que par l'angoisse

---

44. Chenu, Préface to 1942 edition, *La théologie comme science au XIIIe siècle* (Paris: Vrin, 1957), 11.

45. Chenu, 'La psychologie de la foi dans la théologie du XIIIe siècle. Genèse de la doctrine de saint Thomas Somme théologique, IIa IIae, q. 2, a. 1.' (1932) in *La Parole de Dieu I. La Foi dans intelligence* (Paris: Cerf, 1964), 77–104, 88–92.

46. Augustine: '*Fecisti nos ad te, et inquietum est cor nostrum donc requiescat in te.*' *Confessions*, Book I, chap. 1. Chenu glossed that Aquinas' teaching ('*Imperfectio cognitionis est de ratione fidei, ponitur enim in eius definitione.*' ST Ia IIae, q. 67, a.3) was 'moins pathétique mais non moins profonde' ['less pathetic but no less profound'] than Augustine's. 'La Psychologie de la foi', 99.

discrète qu'il recèle: pour saint Thomas, cette inquiétude est
dans la nature même de la foi; c'est par là que la foi se classe
et se définit dans la hiérarchie des assentiments, autant que
par sa certitude: «*Imperfectio cognitionis est de ratione fidei,
ponitur enim in ejus definitione.*» [Ia IIae, q.67, a.3][47]
[The density of the text of the *De Veritate* goes beyond the
most Pascalian of *pensées* in the power of its emotion and
in its religious value; it will only have a reply in the anxious
descriptions of the mystic moving forward in the 'shadows'
of faith. But in the eyes of the theologians, it is valued by the
qualification given to that anxiety, much more than by the
discrete anguish it harbours: for St Thomas this anxiety is *in
the very nature* of faith. This is how faith classifies and defines
itself in the hierarchy of sentiments, as much as through its
certainty: '*Imperfectio cogitationis est de ratione fidei, ponitur
enim in ejus definition.*' (Ia IIae q.67 a.3).]

He found there the ontological warrant for the coherence of human
reason and faith:

Dieu dans son humaine pédagogie, pourra n'éveiller que peu
à peu notre intelligence à une lumière trop éblouissante; mais
dès le début, sous le régime d'autorité que doit accepter tout
disciple, c'est l'intelligence qui abordera le mystère.[48]
[God, in his human pedagogy, could only awaken our
understanding little by little to a light which is too dazzling;
but from the beginning, under the rule of authority which
every disciple must accept, it is understanding which will
approach the mystery.]

Chenu observed in Thomas not merely harmonisation of the seem-
ingly incompatible Aristotelian theory of scientific understanding
and the affective adherence of faith, but evidence of the critical presence of Thomas' own spiritual experience.[49] From Thomas' contem-
plative-scholar life came the evidence for the co-existence of affective
and intuitive elements in the act of faith. This coherence of an 'intuition' [intuition] and a 'mentalité' [mind-set] informed his synthesis.

---

47. 'La Psychologie de la foi', 97.
48. 'La Psychologie de la foi', 95.
49. 'c'est l'âme religieuse de saint Thomas qui la fournit', 96.

L'appétit de béatitude qui détermine son assentiment, loin
d'enclore sa raison dans une sécurité trop courte, provoque
incessamment sa recherche.[50]
[Far from enclosing reason in insufficient safety, the appetite
for beatitude, which determines assent, unceasingly provokes
the search for reason.]

That the profound yearning for knowledge and understanding does
not cancel out faith was an insight grounded in the mentality that
faith and Revelation are not introduced or developed outside of the
laws of our human existence and psychology. Faith is not a divine
overriding of human structures of understanding. Here in the
Angelic Doctor's own teaching was the turn to human experience,
well before the feared Kant. As well, it demonstrated that Thomas had
evaluated the arguments of his antecedents, in a way that resembled
the historical analysis condemned as 'Modernist'. Thomas had incorporated reason into faith. Although each of these propositions was
condemned as erroneous by the modern authorities of neo-scholasticism, Chenu had found they already figured in the master authority,
Thomas Aquinas.

It is significant that Chenu presented Thomas' innovation in such
existential and historical terms. Chenu's *ressourcement* of Aquinas
was as concerned with uncovering the Thomas' human experience as
with determining the genealogy of his theological and philosophical
sources.[51]

In one of a number of his key articles published around 1937,
Chenu examined how faith is both about communion with God and
the formal assent to dogma. This apparent conflict lies at the heart of

---

50. 'c'est l'âme religieuse de saint Thomas qui la fournit', 96.
51. Later Chenu described the method of his *ressourcement* of Aquinas as: 'selon
    toutes les ressources que procure l'application de la méthode à l'étude du texte, de
    la pensée et de la personnalité intellectuelle d'un écrivain.' [according to all the
    resources which enable the application of the method to the study of the text, the
    thought, and the intellectual character of the writer'.] (Archives de la province
    dominicaine de France, Paris, Le Saulchoir—Collège 9 (18)), cited in André
    Duval OP, 'Aux origines de l'«Institut historique d'études thomistes» du Saulchoir
    (1920s.). Notes et Documents', 435. This interest in Aquinas culminated in
    Chenu's own favourite book *St Thomas d'Aquin et la théologie* (1959).

the split between positive and speculative theology.[52] The article was published in *Vie Spirituelle*, so its tone presents a contrast to his usual more polemical style. Faith is a strictly personal way of seeing that assimilates our understanding to God, and is equally a work of the will and love:

> dans cette lumière, mon regard rejoint, découvre avec étonnement celui que Dieu porte luimême sur la vie du monde, sur ma vie à moi; moi dans la destinée mystérieuse du monde, avec ma propre destinée, mystérieuse aussi, en face du Dieu Trinité.
> [in that light my gaze returns and discovers with astonishment the one whom God himself nurtures in the life of the world, in my own life; me in the mysterious destiny of the world, with my own destiny, equally mysterious, in front of God the Trinity.][53]

---

52. There is some suggestion of Blondel's influence in Chenu's interest in the active and experiential view of faith, the rejection of extrinsicism, and also of the implications of Blondel's distinction between immanentism and the immanent principle of human knowing. While Chenu did not directly acknowledge Blondel, he seemed to pursue a parallel quest to Blondel's, identifying within Aquinas' corpus what Blondel constructed at a deliberate distance from the wizened contemporary 'scholasticism' that he despised. Yet later, Congar warned against attributing too much influence on Chenu to Blondel, given Chenu's limited study of modern philosophy. Congar: 'Il ne semble pas que le P. Chenu ait beaucoup fréquenté l'oeuvre de Maurice Blondel, ni connu son «monophorisme»', and 'Bien que n'ayant pas une formation philosophique complète, surtout en philosophie moderne, il avait le goût du problème philosophique.' ['It appears that Fr Chenu was not very familiar with Maurice Blondel's work, and neither was he aware of his "monophorisme"' and 'While he had not received a full philosophical formation, particularly not in modern philosophy, he had a taste for philosophical problems'.] 'Le Père M-D Chenu', in Robert van der Gucht and Herbert Vorgrimler, editors, *Bilan de la théologie du XXe siècle*, volume II (Paris: Casterman, 1970), 772–787, 777, 773. Later Congar admitted he was more influenced by Möhler than Blondel's work on Tradition, even though he cited him: 'J'ai l'habitude—c'est presque une "manie"—de citer des auteurs qui ont dit avant moi ce que je veux dire. Ce ne sont pas toujours des "sources".' ['I have the habit—almost an "obsession"—of citing authors who have already said what I want to say. They are not always "sources".'] Congar, 'Preface' in Charles MacDonald, *Church and World in the Plan of God: Aspects of History and Eschatology in the Thought of Père Yves Congar OP* (Frankfurt: Verlag Peter Lang, 1982).
53. Chenu, 'L'unité de la foi. Réalisme et formalisme' (1937) in *La Parole de Dieu I. La Foi dans intelligence* (Paris: Cerf, 1964), 15. Chenu cited three 'traits' of

In formal terms, faith is an intellectual virtue, socially transmitted and located in the community of faith. There revealed truth is taught across generations, through the Church defining, condemning errors, and affirming the tradition and more contemporary experiences of faith. So faith checks mystical tendencies to solipsism or other-world-liness, and the more general tendency of those captivated to disengage from human reality, to dissociate the inner illumination from its object and source, intuition from the conceptual, the individual from society, and experience from tradition.[54] Chenu identified the issue as the need to restore human understanding as constitutive of faith. To conceive faith exclusively as assent to something extrinsic, as exclusive of human processes of understanding, is a 'fausse exaltation du surnaturel'. The supernatural character of faith is not outside of human experience but inserted intimately in our being according to its human condition. Chenu observed that the unity of faith revolves on the recognition that the divine encounter of faith occurs humanly:

> Dieu prend l'homme tel qu'il est; la foi, aussi, même si l'âme a peu de ressources de connaissance ou d'amour. Réalisme de la foi, oui, mais réalisme humain!
> [God takes man as he finds him, and faith too, even if the soul has few resources of knowledge or love. Realism of faith, yes, but human realism!]

and

> Dans le dynamisme même de la foi est inscrit l'appel de la vision. Mais n'oublions jamais que la garantie même du réalisme de la foi est que notre foi soit toujours HUMAINE.[55]

---

the 'realisme de la foi' [realism of faith]: 'une *perception*'—'Regard attentif, compréhensif' ['a *perception*'—'comprehensive, attentive gaze'] (characterised in the human analogy of the focused gaze of the nursing mother and child); 'une oeuvre de *volonté* et d'*amour*'—'désirée' ['a labour of *will* and *love*'—'desired']; and 'une acte strictement *personnel*'—'personne à personne' [a *strictly personal* action'—'person to person'], 14–15.

54. 'la tentation de dissocier lumière et objet, intuition et notion, individu et société, experience et tradition. La tentation du croyant est de rejeter l'humain, tout l'humain'. ['the temptation to dissociate light and object, intuition and idea, individual and society, experience and tradition. The believer's temptation is to reject the human, everything human'.] 'L'unité de la foi', 17.

55. [Chenu's emphasis] 'L'unité de la foi', 18.

> [The appeal of the vision is written in the very dynamism of
> faith. But never forget that the very guarantee of the realism of
> faith is that our faith is always HUMAN.]

Drawing on Thomas' conviction that faith shares the reality of all
human operations, Chenu proposed a revised theological understanding of humanity. The foundation for this coherence of the
human and divine, faith and reason in the unity of faith is the Word
made flesh, because the Incarnation assures us that all that is human
has been assumed in Christ.

> De même que les actions du Christ sont «théandriques»
> (oeuvres humaines, pleinement humaines, et cependant
> divines), de même, toutes proportions gardées, notre raison,
> et nos concepts, et nos formules dans la foi.[56]
> [Just as Christ's actions are 'theandric' (human works, fully
> human works, and yet also divine), in the same way, relatively,
> are our reason, our concepts, and our formulas of faith
> (theandric).]

The unity of faith, like the divine-human nature of Christ, holds
together without diminishment both the supernatural light of faith
and the action of human understanding through recognising the pat-
terning of faith on the divine mystery it reveals. Chenu resolved the
problem of dualism in faith and theology by reinstating the anthropological condition of faith, and by analogy the role of reason in
constructing theology. This is the earliest explicit christological analogy in Chenu's earlier writings, and encapsulates the grammar of the
Incarnation so characteristic of his later work.

Theology as faith in reason

Chenu's writings between the wars sought to establish the way reason
functions in theology. In 'La théologie comme science au XIIIe siècle'
he traced the growing critical use of reason in medieval theology, as
demonstrated in Thomism's correlation of Christian traditions with

---

56. 'L'unité de la foi', 19.

Aristotelian philosophy.[57] 'Position de la théologie' developed this theological correlation and proposed new bearings for theology from its location in history and how human understanding constitutes theology.[58] In *Une école de théologie: le Saulchoir* Chenu distinguished this critical integration of reason from the introverted rationalism of 'modern scholasticism'. This manifesto of his theological reform of the curriculum at *Le Saulchoir* presented theology as a human 'science'. He thus affirmed that in the interplay of the subjective and objective condition of faith there is coherence between Revelation and human reason. If a theology is to be responsive to the mystery of the Incarnation, it must appreciate the importance of history.[59] In these theological works, Chenu promoted the need for theology to continue a critical correlation with contemporary philosophy, while preaching the truths of Revelation in terms of the historical condition of the human experience of faith.[60]

La théologie comme science au XIIIe siècle

Chenu's early studies on Thomas' doctrine of faith retraced Aquinas' arguments for the integration of philosophy in the construction of theology. In an early demonstration of 'ressourcement', Chenu followed the development of a scientific method in theology, 'la foi in statu scientiae', from thirteenth century scholastic texts. He sought authorisation from Thomas for a more critical theological incorporation of reason, which excluded neither the subjective experience

---

57. 'La théologie comme science au XIIIe siècle. Genèse de la doctrine de Saint Thomas. *Sum. Theol., IaPars, q. 1, art. 2 et 8*', in *Archives d'histoire doctrinale et littéraire du Moyen Age (AHDLMA)*, 2 (1927): 31–71. This article was revised in an unpublished manuscript in 1943 then republished in an expanded version in 1957 as *La théologie comme science au XIIIe siècle* (Paris: Librairie Philosophique J Vrin, 1957).
58. 'Position de la théologie' (1935) in *La Parole de Dieu I. La Foi dans intelligence* (Paris: Cerf, 1964), 115–138.
59. *Une école*, 58–64 [134–139].
60. Chenu later cast this as an ancient and never fully resolved dialectic for Christian theology: 'la curieuse dialectique d'une foi qui, en quête d'éternel, valorise le temps, et d'une raison qui, liée au temps et au lieu, cède à l'éternisme de l'abstraction.' ['the curious dialectic of a faith which, in search of the eternal, values time, and of a reason which, linked to time and place, gives way to the eternalism of abstraction.'] 'Situation humaine: corporalité et temporalité' (1958), 415.

of faith, nor the supernatural nature of faith's inner illumination. He presented Thomas' methodological elaboration of Anselm's 'faith seeking understanding' in the *Summa* as 'l'épisode le plus sensationnel de l'entrée d'Aristote en Chrétienté' ['the most sensational episode of Aristotle's entry into Christianity'], an innovative rupture with all that preceded it rather than the summit of an evolution in medieval theological understanding.[61] Such innovation, what Chenu described as a new sap for theology, offered a precedent for justifying similar changes in contemporary neo-Thomist theology.

'La théologie comme science au XIIIe siècle' (1927) described the genealogy of Aquinas' break with the typological and allegorical expositions of *sacra pagina* that was called *sacra doctrina* in the previous centuries.[62] This study of the background to articles 2 and 8 of the Prologue of Thomas' *Summa theologiae* showed how the various attempts by Aquinas' contemporaries to integrate *expositio* of the scriptural and patristic texts with extra-textual theological speculation had faltered on their fear of diluting Revelation with human reasoning.[63] Propaedeutic use of philosophy in defence of the faith had been condoned well before Aquinas. Twelfth century theologians already debated the rational coherence of theological propositions, but their schemas were not systematised.[64] Some thirteenth century theologians, like Fishacre (d 1248), Kilwardby (d 1261) and Alexander of Hales (d 1241), had used Aristotelian categories in disputa-

---

61. 'Préface', 'La théologie comme science au XIIIe siècle' (1943), reprinted with 1957 preface, 13.
62. Chenu, 'Les Magistri. La "science" theologique' in *La théologie au douzième siècle*, 323–350, especially 329–337; and Chenu, 'La décadence de l'allégorisation. Un témoin: Garnier de Rochefort († v 1200)', in *L'homme devant Dieu: Mélanges offerts au Père Henri de Lubac*, volume II (Paris: Aubier, Éditions Montaigne, 1964), 129–135.
63. *ST* Ia, q.1, a.2: 'Utrum sacra doctrina sit scientia'; a.8: 'Utrum haec doctrina sit argumentativa'.
64. 'La théologie comme science' (1927), 43, 46. Chenu noted approvingly the creative diversity that accompanied the confusion of these theological approaches compared to more recent theology: 'le XIIe siècle présente ici une opulente fécondité que nous dissimule fâcheusement l'uniforme de la scolastique post- tridentine.' ['the 12th century here offers an opulent fruitfulness which the uniformity of post-tridentine scholasticism infuriatingly hides from us'] 'Les Magistri. La "science" theologique', 336. See also *La théologie est- elle une science?* for Chenu's approval of 'Les divers systèmes théologiques' ['the variety of theological systems'] in the history of theology, 99–105.

tion but they limited such inferior rational argument to combat with heretics or unbelievers or to the instruction of the faithful.[65] Chenu concluded that while Kilwardby studied Aristotle, giving an account of the content, procedures and demands of scientific method (*modus artificialis*) in the prologue to his *summa*, he declined to apply this technique to understanding *sacra doctrina*, because he was blocked by an Augustinian mentality that opposed *scientia* (*ratio inferior*) to *sapientia* (*ratio superior*).[66] The function exercised by human reason in theology, for Chenu, was held to be a register of the anthropological awareness and commitment to the human component of faith and correspondingly a measure of his independence from Augustinian suspicions about 'scientia' and the world.

Before Kilwardby, William of Auxerre (d 1231) provided the key to a theological appropriation of scientific methodology by recognising the likeness of the articles of faith to the scientific principles in Aristotle's *Posterior Analytics*.[67] Applying this comparison to *sacra doctrina*, William proposed an objective function for the articles of faith.[68] Chenu judged that, although successive theologians had noted this insight, none expanded on it, and he attributed 'cette pudeur intellectuelle' ['that intellectual modesty'] to an over-concern to protect the supernatural character of faith and Revelation from any mere

---

65. 'La théologie comme science' (1927), 46; *La théologie comme science au XIIIe siècle* (1957), 34.

66. 'La théologie comme science' (1927), 44–46. 'Kilwardby l'accepte, mais en la surchargeant de distinctions qui trahissent la résistance irréductible d'une mentalité augustinienne' [Kilwardby accepts this but does so overloading it with distinctions which betray the irreducible resistance to an Augustinian mind-set'] (1927), 36; and 'Il y a là évidemment autre chose qu'une non-distinction sur le mot reçu de *doctrina sacra* et sur son contenu, dont l'hétérogénéité n'apparaîtrait pas. Il y a une implicite répugnance à admettre dans le domaine de cette donné révélé l'intervention, ou mieux le principe même de l'intervention propre de la raison.' ['Here there is clearly something other than a non-distinction on the received meaning and content of *doctrina sacra*, whose heterogenerity would not appear. There is an implicit loathing for allowing intervention, or rather, the principle of the intervention which is proper to reason, to enter the domain of the revealed data.'] 'La théologie comme science' (1927), 46. (*cf* also, 57). A fuller treatment is presented in 'Ratio superior et inferior. Un cas de philosophie chrétienne', in *Revue des sciences philosophiques et théologiques*, XXIX (1940): 84–89.

67. 'La théologie comme science' (1927), 49–52.

68. 'La théologie comme science' (1927), 51–52.

human analysis.[69] He added pointedly that this is the problem of the Augustinians of all eras.[70] Chenu asserted that Thomas' method and conception of theology as 'science' was not only a leap beyond the understanding of these previous attempts, but marked a new 'discovery' of humanity, an advance in creaturely self-understanding. Chenu interpreted Aquinas' contribution as a dynamic and revolutionary interaction of the 'donné' ['data'] of Revelation and faith and the human 'construit' ['construct'] of reason and understanding, which provided the moment of dialectical resolution when the opposites of contemplation in faith and Aristotelian 'scientific method' were united.[71] Theology as science, as intellectual faith, enhanced humanity's inherent connaturality with God in a preview of our beatific destiny.[72] Later Chenu would cite the Tübingen theologian Johann Evangelist Kuhn's epigram to capture the ramifications of such innovation: 'Pas de théologie, sans nouvelle naissance.' ['No theology without new birth.']⁷³

---

69. 'Indice révélateur de cette pudeur intellectuelle dans ces esprits tout pénétrés de saint Augustin, ils ont recours, pour qualifier et définir leur amoureuse recherche, au concept augustinienne de *sapientia*, qui, à leurs yeux, se changeait d'affectivité et de dévotion, en même temps qu'il éliminait la dialectique intempérante et le goût terrestre qui sont l'apanage de la *scientia*.' ['A revealing indication of that intellectual modesty in those minds which were completely permeated with St Augustine, to describe and define their beloved research they resort to the Augustinian concept of *sapientia*, which in their eyes resolved affectivity and devotion at the same time as it eliminated intemperate dialectic and the earthly taste which are the prerogative of *scientia*.'] (1927), 57. Chenu indicted this as a 'réserve spontanée, comme une timidité, en face de la vérité révélée et de la réalité.' ['spontaneous reservation, like a timidity, in the face of revealed truth and reality.'] 'La théologie comme science' (1927), 56.
70. 'La théologie comme science' (1927), 34.
71. 'Beau témoignage d'une synthèse très parfaitement une entre la mystique du croyant et la science du théologien, que cette théorie de la subalternation des sciences, qui, légitimant d'une part l'établissement de la dialectique en terrain de révélation, rattache d'autre part toute cette dialectique à la science même de Dieu, *scientia Dei et beatorum*.' ['This theory of the subalternation of the sciences which, on the one hand legimates the establishment of dialectic in the field of revelation, on the other hand joins all this dialectic to the very science of God, *scientia Dei et beatorum*, is a wonderful testimony of a synthesis which is perfectly one between the believer's mysticism and the science of the theologian.'] 'La théologie comme science' (1927), p. 70.
72. 'La théologie comme science' (1927), 63.
73. 'Position de la théologie' (1935), 115–138, (115).

William of Auxerre's analogy of the articles of faith with the principles of science was the first application of the theory of subalternation of one science to another to *sacra doctrina*. According to this theory, a science (or body and method of knowledge) can be verified by the relationship of its content and mode of knowledge to another higher science, in terms of this science's verifiable principles. The lesser science becomes intrinsic to the higher one by being drawn up into its principles. The theory of subalternation of sciences explains how theology can be a 'science' even as it depends on principles or truths that are not self-evident or open to empirical confirmation. Initially even Thomas in his early commentary on the *Sentences* had failed to explain how the articles of faith are not self-evident except to the believer, because he had limited subalternation to faith not theology.[74] Chenu stressed his discovery only emerged in the later commentary on Boethius' *De trinitate* and his more conclusive *Summa* treatment. Thomas recognised that theology's inability to establish evidence for its claims is no different to the derivative qualities of other branches of human knowledge. He found Bonaventure's use of 'subalternation' still restricted to the subordination of theology to Scripture. Yet it held the key to applying William of Auxerre's analogy. Aquinas argued that as optics to geometry is subordinate, or music to arithmetic, so theology is a subordinate 'science' which through faith receives its principles from the revealed higher 'science' of God's self-knowledge. So, theology deduces both its method and content from the higher science of God.[75] Because evidence for the articles of faith is afforded by the higher 'science', the 'science' of God, then reason is no longer limited to providing proofs for the articles of faith. Instead, the role of reason in the 'science' of theology is to deduce, from these articles of faith, further understanding of the truth of Revelation. The article of faith is no longer the matter or subject of theological exposition and research, as in twelfth century understanding of *sacra doctrina*, but the principle already known, from which theology works for further understanding.

> L'article de foi trouve son «lieu» dans l'immense genèse de vérité qui va de Dieu, Vérité première, à la modeste conclusion théologique: la théorie de la science qui semblait devoir à

---

74. Chenu cited: *I Sentences*, Prologue, a. 2, obj. 2; a. 5, ad. 4 in (1927), 34, 59.
75. *ST* Ia, q. 1, a. 2.

jamais consacrer l'hétérogénéité de la lumière divine de la
foi avec la laborieuse et humaine spéculation du théologien,
en souligne au contraire, sous les distinctions nécessaires, la
féconde continuité.
[The article of faith finds its 'locus' in the huge genesis of truth
which comes from God, the first Truth, to theology's modest
conclusion: the theory of science which seems to always have
had to dedicate the heterogeneity of the divine light of faith
with the laborious human speculation of the theologian,
which on the contrary, with the necessary distinctions,
emphasises the fruitful continuity.][76]

Chenu found that subalternation resolved for Thomas any apparent
contradiction between the speculative task of understanding faith,
particularly the development of faith, and the contemplative simplicity of faith. Reason is declared not heterogeneous to revealed truth,
but is 'une remontée de la foi vers la science de Dieu et la première
étape sur la voie de la vision béatifique, *scientia dei et beatorum*' ['an
ascent of faith towards the science of God and the first stage on the
journey to the beatific vision, *scientia dei et beatorum*'].[77]

In the later editions of *La théologie comme science au XIIIe siècle*,
further implications of this subalternation are outlined. Faith is presented as constitutive of theology. In subalternation it is faith that
provides the necessary continuity between the 'science of God' and
the critical human operation of theology, thereby preserving transcendence while validating human reason as not extrinsic to theology.[78] Theology is a science by the same means that it is mystical;

---

76. 'La théologie comme science' (1927), 63; *La théologie comme science au XIIIe
    siècle* (1957), 74.
77. 'La théologie comme science' (1927), 63.
78. 'Non seulement par conséquent livraison d'un donné, d'une série de propositions
    acceptées d'autorité, par une légitime «obéissance» intellectuelle à Dieu se
    révélant, mais continuité organique, psychologique et religieuse, selon laquelle
    la lumière de foi, émanation de la lumière divine dans l'esprit de l'homme,
    compose le milieu indispensable à la connaissance des propositions révélées.'
    ['Not only, therefore, delivery a fact or a series of propositions accepted through
    authority, through legitimate intellectual 'obdience' to God who reveals himself,
    but an organic, psychological, and religious continuity, according to which the
    light of faith, the emanation of the divine light in the human mind, makes up
    the indispensable environment for the knowledge of revealed propositions.'] *La
    théologie comme science au XIIIe siècle* (1957), 73.

subalternation also explained the integral role of the mystical dimension of theology.[79] Confidence in the *intellectus fidei* offered Chenu further demonstration of Thomas' ubiquitous application of the principle of the unity between human understanding of Revelation and the way all things are known humanly: 'cognita sunt in cognoscente secundum modum cognoscentis' (*ST* IIa IIae, q. 1, a. 2).[80] Chenu had already linked the legitimacy of argument in theology with the scholastic axiom, '*Gratia non tollit naturam, sed perficit*'. Chenu observed that Aquinas' favourite axiom found its highest and most fruitful realisation in this subalternation.[81] Yet Chenu observed, the theory cannot completely account for the discrepancy between the relationship of the believer to God, and to that of a physicist to a mathematician. So by the 1943 and 1957 editions Chenu had added that theology's relationship to the 'science of God' is the 'quasi-subalternation' of an imperfect 'science'.[82] Subalternation reinforced the conviction that the object of faith is God, and not doctrinal conclusions. This allowed Chenu to insist more on the subjective-objective dynamic of theology, that the end of theology is to know God through Revelation and faith, emphasising more clearly than he had before the place of scripture in theology.[83] By locating theology as a science, albeit subalternated, he implied that theology is necessarily concerned with the whole of reality, not merely with specific religious subjects at the periphery of human affairs, which had become its constricted charter under modernity.[84]

---

79. *La théologie comme science* (1957), 73–4.
80. *La théologie comme science* (1957), 71, 70 n 1.
81. 'La théologie comme science' (1927), 64–5.
82. *a théologie comme science* (1957), 80–85
83. Chenu emphasised medieval scholasticism's basis in scripture in the opening of his chapter on 'The dialectic of science' with: 'La théologie est la science d'un livre, le livre des livres, la Bible. Elle l'est de droit, car, science de Dieu, elle trouve dans ce livre la parole de Dieu, la révélation de Dieu.' ['Theology is the science of a book, the book of books, the Bible. It is rightly so since, as the science of God, it finds the revelation of God in this book of the word of God.'] *La théologie comme science* (1957), 15. *Cf* also 13–14, 16–17.
84. *La théologie comme science* (1957), 100. *Cf* also 'On ne manquera pas de donner à cette «continuité», objective et subjective, sa portée épistémologique, si on observe la densité de la *continuatio* dans l'univers—non aristotélicien en cela, certes—de saint Thomas, comme principe d'être et d'intelligibilité des choses, que ce soit en physique, en psychologie des facultés dans l'homme, en analyse de l'action et de la causalité, même instrumentale', 73, n 1. ['We will not fail

The 1927 article drew some discussion, and its subsequent editions continue to be cited in debates on the nature of theology and the meaning of Thomas' treatise on *sacra doctrina*.[85] It is significant that even in subsequent editions, Chenu did not modify his judgment that Thomas' theory of subalternation radically outstepped all previous understanding of 'theology as science'. This contrasted markedly with more evolutionary readings of the development of doctrine, which vindicate passive or only gradual doctrinal and method- ological change. For Chenu Aquinas pre-figured and legitimised the orthodoxy of innovative reform in the critical practice of theology. An early critic of this interpretation was the Franciscan Jean-François Bonnefoy, who was concerned that Chenu had mistakenly attributed Bonaventure's contribution to Aquinas, giving Thomas sole credit for the scientific status of theology. While Chenu registered Bonnefoy's criticism in the 1943 edition's preface, he did not address Bonnefoy's arguments.[86] In the 1927 original version Chenu's case for Aquinas' innovation depended on a detailed account of Fishacre and Kilwardby. Its sparse treatment of Bonaventure's use of subalternation led to a focus on Thomas' later works that over-emphasised Aquinas' contribution, while playing down his earlier minimal reading of

---

to give this objective and subjective "continuity" its epistemological import, if we observe the denseness of *continuatio* in the universe—non-Aristotelian, of course—of St Thomas, as the principle of being and of understanding of things, whether in physics, in the psychology of human facutlies, in the analysis of action and causality, even if this be instrumental.'] 'Position', 120: '«Le Verbe s'est fait chair»: ma foi en raisonnant contemple volontiers en cette «chair» tout ce que comporte une humanité, depuis une sensibilité soumise à la tentation jusqu'à une intelligence ouverte à la vision de Dieu; et ma raison, *sub lumine fidei*, se charge de résoudre les délicates questions que pose, jusque dans les mots, une pareille révélation.' ['"The Word was made flesh": in reasoning, my faith willingly contemplates in this "flesh" everything which makes up humanity, from the sensitivity subjected to temptation to understanding which is open to the vision of God; and my reason, *sub lumine fidei*, takes charge of resolving the delicate questions which such a revelation raises, even in the words.']

85. Chenu's noted at the beginning of Preface to XIII and note 2 articles on it by: M Grabmann, 'De theologia ut scientia argumentativa secundum S Albertum magnum et S Thomam Aquinum', in *Angelicum*, XIV (1937): 39–60; Jean-François Bonnefoy OFM, 'La théologie comme science et l'application de la Foi selon S Thomas d'Aquin', in *Ephemerides theologicae louvainienses*, XIV (1937): 421–446, and 600–631; XV (1938): 491–516.

86. 'Préface', (1943), reprinted with (1957) preface, 11, n 2.

subalternation in the *Commentary on the Sentences*. Following the detailed attention to Kilwardby and Fishacre, the reader is stopped short by the light treatment of the Franciscan's contribution by Chenu.[87] In the 1943 and 1957 editions Chenu did expand on this shorter article, including Bonaventure's input, but Chenu did not revise his argument or respond to its critics. There was his acknowledgment of an over-emphasis on confining the scientific character of theology to the deduction of conclusions from the articles of faith and he cited Congar's arguments for a univocal meaning for *sacra doctrina*, but left his own equivocal interpretation unrevised.[88]

This revival by Chenu of the importance of the theory of subalternation is credited with initiating the twentieth century engagement of theology with 'earthly realities'. This led to the theological disputes with '*Konklusiontheologie*', which came to define the innovation of the 'nouvelle théologie'.[89] Yet his interpretation of the meaning of *sacra doctrina* in the first Part of the *Summa* has generated much controversy.[90] In two comprehensive deconstructions of Chenu's exegeti-

---

87. 'Saint Bonaventure avait bien, il est vrai, d'une subordination de la théologie à l'Écriture; mais il s'agissait d'une simple dépendance de fait, en dehors de tout souci de systématisation, puisque chez lui le problème de la «science» n'était pas vraiment posé.' ['St Bonaventure, it is true, subordinated theology to Scripture; but this was a case of a simple subordination of fact, beyond any desire of systematisation, since for him the problem of "science" did not really arise.'] 'La théologie comme science' (1927), 63 and '[Bonaventure] s'agit de subordination au sens commun du mot, non cet agencement technique en vertu duquel une science reçoit d'une autre les «principes» de son raisonnement', 55 ['Bonaventure used subordination in the common sense of the word, and not in that technical use thanks to which one science receives the "principles" of its reasoning from another.'].

88. *La théologie comme science au XIIIe siècle* (1957), 78–80.

89. Two more recent examples published in English are: Piet Schoonenberg SJ, 'The Theologian's Calling, Freedom, and Constraint' in *Authority in the Church*, edited by Piet Fransen SJ (Leuven: K.U Leuven Press, 1983), 92–118, 93: 'Chenu's article remains modern because of what he writes concerning faith, the tie between heaven and earth, and its influence upon theology.'; and Roger Haight SJ, *Dynamics of Theology* (New York: Paulist Press, 1990), 2. Chenu's criticised the reduction of theology to 'a science of conclusions' in 'La littérature comme "lieu" de la théologie', in *Revue des sciences philosophiques et théologiques*, LIII (1969): 70–80, 73.

90. Marie-Joseph Congar OP, in *Bulletin thomiste*, 5/8 (1938): 490–505; Victor White OP, *Holy Teaching: The Idea of Theology according to St Thomas Aquinas* (London: Blackfriars Publications, 1958); James A Weisheipl OP, 'Review: *Is Theology a Science?*', in *New Scholasticism*, XXXV (1961): 241–243; James A Weisheipl OP,

cal and historical arguments, Henry Donneaud OP accuses him of lacking a true historical-critical discipline, not being objective about his sources, and failing in the humility required to revise his faulty conclusions.[91] These are serious charges against a work which was so foundational for Chenu's theology and his historical credentials. Donneaud judges that Chenu applied 'une clef de lecture reçue *a priori*' [a key of the received *a priori* reading] to discard the univocal meaning for *sacra doctrina* for article 2, in favour of the anachronistic twentieth century meaning of 'theological science'. He also finds that Aquinas' extrapolation from Bonaventure's 'sub-alternation', in the commentary on the *Sentences*, did not sufficiently distinguish between scripture as *sacra doctrina* and the critical understanding of Revelation that defined 'theology as science' in the later works. Chenu acknowledged that this was not a full exegetical study.[92] Donneaud convincingly argues that his genetic historical method was inadequate as Chenu needed to examine more the relevant texts in Aquinas, instead of his antecedents.[93] Chenu's account, in the 1927 original, of the reference to sub-alternation in the *Commentary on the Sentences* does suggest that the rupture in the understanding of theology as science claimed for Aquinas' later works may be less clear than he asserted.[94] Yet Chenu's explanation for the halt- ing progress of the other thirteenth century masters' understanding of the scientific nature of theology does not necessarily depend on the discontinuity he proposed between Aquinas' early and later works. Despite the proximity of Bonaventure's use of sub-alternation, his later rejection of Aquinas' theology clearly distinguished his understanding from

---

'The Meaning of *Sacra Doctrina* in *Summa Theologiae* I, q.1', in *The Thomist*, 38 (1974); Michel Corbin SJ, *Le Chemin de la théologie chez Thomas d'Aquin* (Paris: Beauchesne, 1974); John I Jenkins CSC, *Knowledge and Faith in Thomas Aquinas* (Cambridge: Cambridge University Press, 1997).

91. Henry Donneaud OP, 'Histoire d'une histoire: M-D Chenu et «La théologie comme science au XIIIe siècle»', in *Mémoire Dominicaine*, 4, (1994): 139–175, and 'M-D Chenu et l'exégèse de *Sacra Doctrina*', in *Revue des sciences philosophiques et théologiques*, 81 (1997): 415–437.

92. 'N'ayant pas ici à présenter une exégèse textuelle suivie, mais à discerner les points critiques de l'évolution doctrinale': ['Not presenting a sustained textual exegesis here, but discerning the critical points of doctrinal development.'] Chenu, 'La théologie comme science' (1927), 61.

93. Donneaud, (1997), 422.

94. 'La théologie comme science' (1927), 58–60.

the correlation with philosophical method that sub-alternation generated for Aquinas.

Donneaud does register that Chenu was really answering article 2 even though this discussion is presented instead as an answer to article 1: 'what is *sacra doctrina*?' Donneaud identifies Chenu's 'clef de lecture' ['reading key'] as stemming from an unexamined reception through his teachers Gardeil and Garrigou-Lagrange of John of St Thomas' equivocal interpretation of *sacra doctrina* in the Prima Pars.[95] But he also charges Chenu with having a transparent Hegelian agenda, manifested in the stress on conflict and his dialectical portrayal of Aqui- nas' incorporation of scientific method in theology.[96] Both charges are feasible. Chenu's theological interest and the object of his concern was to relativise the scientific claims of 'modern scholasticism' against Aquinas' more nuanced ascription of *sacra doctrina* broadly to holy teaching *and* the theology that is derived from it. Chenu argued for the 'theology' reading of *sacra doctrina* more in terms of his understanding of the unity of the relationship of doctrine to faith. He held that *sacra doctrina* meant 'theology' (in the modern sense of the word) because of his need to distinguish neo-scholasticism's uncritical alignment of theological reason with rationalism. This was in contrast to the Thomists of the eighteenth century, influenced by Wolffian rationalism, who reduced *sacra doctrina* to theorems which were deduced independently of faith and contemplation on the Word of God.[97] Donneaud observes that for Chenu: 'La connaissance humaine ne culmine pas dans la *ratio* et ses procédés dialectiques, mais dans *l'intellectus*, c'est-à-dire dans la saisie intellective de son objet.'['Human knowledge does not culminate in *ratio* and its dialectical processes but in *intellectus* that is, the intellectual grasp of the object.'][98] The issue for Chenu was that human understanding requires critical reasoning in theology, not the mechanical neo-scholastic rationalism. This was grounded in his confidence in the intellectual condition of faith and theology. Donneaud finds that Chenu's

---

95. A Gardeil OP, *Le donné révélé et la théologie* (Juvisny: Les Éditions du Cerf, 1932), 250; R Garrigou-Lagrange OP, *De Deo Uno: Commentarium in Primam Partem S. Thomae* (Paris: Éditions du Cerf, 1938), 26–145, as cited in Weisheipl, 'The Meaning of *Sacra Doctrina* in *Summa Theologiae* I, q.1', 60–61
96. Donneaud, (1997), 419, 421, 423.
97. Chenu, *La théologie est-elle une science?*, 88–89.
98. Donneaud, (1994), 162.

antagonism to neo-Augustinian separation of faith and reason over-whelmed his scholarship.[99] Whether this sensitivity compromised Chenu's historical objectivity is surely as debatable as the possibility of objectivity itself. Chenu often referred in his later writing to the competing dialectic of these positions in the history of theology, indi-cating his preference while insisting that both are necessary because of the tension between immanence and transcendence in Christiani-ty.[100] As he would later assert:

> Sous ce choc épistémologique, c'est un vieux problème qui nous est posé. Saint Thomas, dans une conjoncture culturelle analogue, se faisait déjà cette objection à l'*unité* du savoir théologique: Comment tenir sous le même registre le Créateur et la créature?[101]
> [Beneath the epistemological shock we are faced with the old problem. In similar cultural circumstances, St Thomas was already objecting to the *unity* of theological knowledge: how could the Creator and the creature be held in the same register?']

That Chenu failed to amend his interpretation even after Congar's cor-rection defies any adequate justification, although some explanation may be found in the proximity of the second edition to his condem-nation in 1942. The 1943 version added a note of acknowledgment to both Gardeil and Garrigou-Lagrange, despite his recent humiliation

---

99. 'Sans doute M-D Chenu garde une réserve spontanée envers les tendances dualistes qui traversent la pensée augustinienne et la rendent selon lui, incapable de saisir, dans une même synthèse, vérités divines et éternelles d'une part (sagesse), réalités temporelles et contingentes d'autre part (science). Une certaine méfiance à l'égard de l'augustinisme accompagnera d'ailleurs toute son oeuvre.' ['M.-D. Chenu probably had spontaneous reservations about the dualist tendencies which run through Augustine's thought and, according to Chenu, make it impossible to hold divine and eternal truths (wisdom) on the one hand, and temporal and contingent realities (science) on the other, in a single synthesis. A certain suspicion towards Augustinianism also goes along with his work.'] Donneaud, (1994), 152.

100. Chenu, *La théologie est-elle une science?*, 103–4 and 'Vérité et liberté dans la foi du croyant' (1959) in *La Parole de Dieu I. La Foi dans intelligence* (Paris: Cerf, 1964), 337–359.

101. Chenu, 'Définition de l'unité de l'enseignement', in *Seminarium,* XXIII/2 (1971): 267–279, 268.

by the latter.[102] Was this failure to revise his position an attempt to establish the orthodoxy of his theology by its overt conformity on *sacra doctrina* with these luminaries of neo-scholasticism? Or was it a stubborn refusal to recant what he regarded as a foundational study for the reform of theology? There is a faint echo of such tenacity in a later related context, the preface to a 1968 French translation of the *Summa theologiae*. Chenu recalled how Aquinas was initially rejected then systematically forgotten, despite his official revival and honours, because of the risk inherent in incorporating reason in theology, and he ends with the battle-cry: 'Il est temps de reprendre l'opération.'['It is time to resume operations!']¹⁰³ Chenu's later works do tend to maintain the equivocal interpretation while paradoxically insisting on the 'unity' of *sacra doctrina*.[104] His objective was to establish the importance that Aquinas had given to understanding theology as scientific and its correlation to reason, more than answering the other articles about *sacra doctrina*. Whether Chenu was not convinced that Congar's work demolished his whole argument remains unknown. Could Chenu have regarded his own work as historical, that is not the definitive work on *sacra doctrina*, but a seminal 'événement' ['event'], to be superseded by the scholarship of his student and colleague, and not subject-matter for continuous revision unlike a textbook would be?¹⁰⁵ It can only be concluded that Chenu's aim to legitimate contemporary theological innovation as consistent with his portrayal of Aquinas' revolution was his overarching concern in the theological climate that preceded Vatican II.[106]

---

102. 'Préface', 'La théologie comme science au XIIIe siècle' (1943), reprinted with (1957) preface, 12, n 1.

103. Chenu, 'Préface', in *Somme theeologique. La théologie: la Prologue et question 1*, translated by HD Gardeil OP (Paris: Éditions du Cerf/ Desclée, 1968): 5–9, 8.

104. These include reference to Congar's article in: 'Définition de l'unité de l'enseignement', 276.

105. Donneaud applauds Congar's detailed and erudite method as much in judgement against Chenu's. Donneaud, (1997), 428.

106. There are further discussions and disputes with other parts of Chenu's groundbreaking work on Thomas Aquinas, especially that on the plan of the *Summa* and Chenu's *exitus-reditus* schema. As these do not touch directly on the anthropological topic I have not discussed them here. See Rudi Te Velde, *Aquinas on God: The 'Divine Science' of the Summa Theologiae* (Farnham: Ashgate, 2006), 10–15.

'La nouvelle théologie'

When in 1935 he published 'Position de la théologie', advocating reform of neo-Thomist theological method, Chenu intensified his historical critique of 'modern scholasticism'.[107] He had expressed his dissatisfaction with the authority bestowed in contemporary theological discourse on Denzinger's *Enchiridion*, which gave this handbook equivalent status to Thomas' theology.[108] 'Position de la théologie' took this criticism further by proposing how theology could be reformed from its theological and philosophical foundations with 'new' bearings for constructing a theology, later to be known as '*la nouvelle théologie*'. While in a less polemical and caustic format than *Une école de théologie: le Saulchoir* which launched his renewal of theological method, this article marks a significant departure from its *ressourcement* antecedents. Congar recalled its origins in an encounter with Chenu before *Le Saulchoir* moved nearer to Paris, where they conspired in 'un accord profond, à la fois intellectuel, vital and apostolique' [a profound agreement, which was intellectual, vital, and apostolic'] to undertake the 'liquidation de la théologie{baroque}' [the liquidation of baroque theology']. They planned their respective tasks. 'Ce fut un moment d'intense et totale concordance des esprits.'[It was a time of intense, total agreement of minds.][109] The plan was not to overturn one set of theological theses for another, Congar insisted, but to propagate a retrieval of the innovation and evangelical intensity of the Thomist tradition. The conspiracy had immediate if not the desired effect. On publishing its manifesto *Une école de théologie: le Saulchoir*, Chenu was condemned for discrediting Thomism and dishonouring Aquinas.[110]

---

107. Chenu, 'Position de la théologie' (1935). Surprisingly it was commended by Garrigou-Lagrange although he condemned *Une école de théologie: le Saulchoir*. Garrigou later regretted as too favourable his letter to Chenu about 'Position'. Étienne Fouilloux, 'Autour d'une mise à l'Index', 34, n 3.

108. From Chenu's review of some introductions to theology in *Revue des sciences philosophiques et théologiques* 24 (1935): 705–7.

109. Yves Congar OP, 'Le frère que j'ai connu' in C Geffré, *L'Hommage differé au Père Chenu* (Paris: Cerf, 1990), 239–245, 242.

110. Père Parente (1942): 'ce discrédit retombe sur saint Thomas.' ['this disrepute falls on St Thomas'] cited by Chenu in his preface to 'La théologie comme science au XIIIe siècle' (1943).

'Position de la théologie' still rings like a declaration of this pro-jected offensive. Its epigram from Johann Kuhn and the dedication to Matthias Scheeben provocatively enlisted the Tübingen reformers as proto-collaborators in this campaign.[111] Chenu's invocation of them situated this article as transitional. It stood between their neo-scho-lastic reinstatement of the intellectual dynamic in Aquinas' doctrine of faith and the historical direction of Chenu's theological curriculum outlined in *Une école de théologie: le Saulchoir*. The more positivist 'return to the sources' method, associated with Congar and Lubac, was described by their opponents as 'la nouvelle théologie', with the pejorative sense that innovation carried for an immutable system.[112] The 'Conclusion theology', that summarised the rationalist analysis of Thomas into propositions bearing the status of articles of faith, had made its object merely the 'principles' of a method rather than the divine reality that these propositions were intended to communicate. 'Modern scholasticism' objectified its intellectualism into a rational-ist creed. Chenu's project attempted an interplay between object and subject in theology that was more true to Thomas' methodology, while it acknowledged the necessary subjectivity demanded by mod-ern psychology. This study of Thomas, uncovered by these innova-tors, exposed this rationalist theology of 'modern-scholasticism' as the actual innovation:

> Le comble du paradoxe sera de voir des théologiens tenir
> que la théologie peut se construire hors l'expérience de foi.
> Théologie mort-née, spéculations à vide, et, à la lettre, sans
> objet.[113]
> [The height of the paradox would be to see theologians
> maintain that theology can be constructed outside of the
> experience of faith. A still-born theology, empty speculation
> and, literally, without object.]

---

111. Avec eux, c'est la liquidation de la «théologie baroque» qui commence.' ['With them began the liquidation of "baroque theology".'] 'Position de la théologie', 'Notes documentaires', 137. He also referred to his debt to Gardeil and Garrigou-Lagrange, 138.
112. Contemporary with this period of Chenu's output were Lubac's *Catholicisme* (1938) and *Surnaturel* (1946), and Congar's *Chrétiens désunis* (1937) and *Esquisses du Mystère de l'Église* (1941).
113. 'Position', 118.

In 'Position de la théologie' Chenu announced the terms of this reform in theological method. He rehearsed the topics of his earlier discussions on the scientific status of theology, that theology has a quasi-scientific mode explained by the theory of subalterna- tion, insisting on the supernatural dimension of Revelation and the incarnation of the divine in the theological work of human reason. Collected together under another citation of Thomas' principle of epistemological continuity, these topics reiterated the human condi-tion of faith and the perception of Revelation: 'Si vraiment l'homme connaît Dieu, il le connaîtra humainement.'['If man really knows God, he knows him humanly'.][114]

Then Chenu focused on the reform of theological method in the section, 'La construction de la théologie', by distinguishing the givens of Revelation, which privileges the object of theology, divine reality as revealed, over dogmatic conclusions; and how the speculative con- struct extrapolates from these revealed givens. The 'donné' is revealed, unlike the givens acquired as extrinsic data in human sciences, but more like the natural law that corresponds to the codified laws of society.[115] The God revealed by Revelation is more interior to humans than we are to ourselves.[116] The construct composed from this data of Revelation is always dependent on it to provide the frame through which the content of Revelation can be understood. Dogmatic formulae are constructed within the limitations of particular times, places and societies, which never equate with or exhaust the full meaning of Revelation. This distinction privileged revealed data, over the speculative formulation, in relation to the object of faith. It also steered between excessively subjective or extrinsicist theologies of Revelation. In this understanding of the Thomist anthropological dynamic, the divine imprint created in human nature corresponds with contemplation of the divine source of Revelation, otherwise Revelation about God would be humanly inaccessible. The unity

---

114. 'Position', 119.
115. Chenu used François Gény's juridical analogy from *Science et technique en droit privé positif* (Paris: L Tenin, 1914), 95 ff: 'la loi inscrite dans la nature même de l'homme individuel ou social, avant qu'un pouvoir positif en ait fixé les inclinations et déterminé les applications concrètes'. ['the law written in the very nature of the individual or social person, before a positive power has fixed its inclinations and determined its concrete applicactions.'] 'Position', 124.
116. 'Position', 123.

of theology is thus preserved through its supernatural source and end. For Chenu human subjectivity is integral to theology and faith because it is there that God meets us.[117] Theology is constructed on *both* the '*donné*' ['data'] and the '*construit*' ['construct'].[118] Chenu asserted that theology requires the historical 'retour aux expériences premières' ['return to the first experiences'] to test the value of any deduced abstract propositions. This implied that only a *ressourcement* of the experiential and historical sources of theology could overcome the stagnation produced by a concentration on metaphysics and the deduction of abstract formulations.[119] Positive and speculative theology should no longer be maintained separately, as Chenu later commented: 'le dépassement du dualisme théologie positive et théologie speculative, qui, dès le début, lorsque j'y avais recours comme tout le monde, me blessait dans mon *intellectus fidei*.' ['the overshoot of the dualism between positive theology and speculative theology which, from the start, when I came across it like everyone else, wounded me in my *intellectus fidei*.'][120]

Chenu broke from his neo-scholastic background to situate the construction of theology within the historical consciousness of modernity. In order to explain how the construct always remains secondary to Revelation, Chenu introduced the role of historical development in theology, as the counter and corrective of 'l'impuissance de la spéculation' ['the powerlessness of speculation']. He concluded that Christian theology is ontologically historical. Historical method, he maintained, was apposite to a faith founded on Revelation in history. While Chenu's understanding of historical development here reflects Hegelian and Bergsonian ideas of progress, he insisted:

---

117. 'Position', 123–126.
118. Chenu presented this unity as incarnationally verified: 'rejeter la seconde, avec ses espoirs et ses efforts d'intelligibilité, hors la zone de la première, ce serait manquer de réalisme, car si Dieu consent à se livrer à la raison humaine, c'est, après l'avoir habilitée, en acceptant la loi native de cette raison.' ['rejecting the latter, with its hopes and attempts at intelligibility, outwith the zone of the former, would be lacking in realism, for if God consents to surrender to human reason it is in accepting the natural law of that reason, having authorised it.'] 'Position', 116.
119. 'Position', 124.
120. Chenu, 'Préface' in Claude Geffré OP, Un *Nouvel Age de la Théologie*, (Paris: Cerf, 1972), 9.

Mais le théologien, lui, travaille sur une histoire. Son «donné», ce ne sont les natures des choses ni leurs formes intemporelles; ce sont des événements, répondant à une *économie*, dont la réalisation est liée au temps, comme l'étendue est liée au corps, par-dessus l'ordre des essences. Le monde réel est celui-là, et non pas l'abstraction du philosophe.[121]
['But the theologian works on a history. His 'givens' are not the nature of things or their timeless forms, but events which respond to an *economy*, whose realisation is linked to time, just as extent is linked to the body, beyond the order of essences. The real world is this one, not the abstraction of philosophy.']

The economy of salvation is revealed in the historical contingencies of creation, incarnation and redemption, and the mission of Christ continued through his mystical body, the Church.[122] Chenu declared that the purpose of theology is contemplation of this sacred history from each theologian's particular place in history, not the deduction from atemporal principles, for the mystery is only recognised in history.[123] This represented a direct attack on the prevailing theological preoccupation with examining eternal causes.[124] To support his claim, Chenu introduced an analogy between the correlation of historical and theological method and the Incarnation of Christ.

Voici à nouveau la «position» de la théologie. Sachant assumer dans cette vision chrétienne du monde l'ordre des natures, tout comme le Christ a assumé une nature humaine, elle reconnaît dans la raison une lumière issue de la pensée divine, que le don nouveau de la foi intègre en son labeur.[125]

---

121. 'Position', 128.
122. 'Position', 130.
123. Later, Chenu captured this in one of his characteristic aphorisms: 'Le Mystère est dans l'histoire. L'Église est dans le monde.' ['The Mystery is in history. The Church is in the world.'] Chenu, 'Histoire du salut et historicité de l'homme dans le renouveau de la théologie' in L Shook and GM Bertrand, editors, *La théologie du renouveau* (Paris: Cerf, 1968), 21–32, 26.
124. 'La théologie est *réaliste*, parce qu'elle est l'intelligence de l'ordre du salut dans son histoire et sa réalisation concrète.' ['Theology is *realistic* because it is the understanding of the economy of salvation in its history and concrete realisation.'] 'Position', 131.
125. 'Position', 129.

[Here once again is the 'position' of theology. Knowing how to assume the order of natures into this Christian vision of the world, just as Christ assumed human nature, it recognises in reason a light which issues from divine thought, which the new gift of faith integrates into its labours.]

Enlisting first Aquinas then surprisingly Augustine as prototypes of historically grounded theology, Chenu concluded that the historical 'givens' of Revelation, which herald the economy of salvation, are components for the construction of theology.[126]

Having dismissed the position that protected the supernatural end of faith and theology from contamination by the human condition, Chenu completed his map of the construction of theology by providing a demonstration of history as a locus for theological reflection. The human condition of the theological enterprise was based in Aquinas' teaching on the theological virtues. Rejecting Peter Lombard's insistence on a direct unmediated infusion of grace by the Holy Spirit, Aquinas declared virtue to be rational, located not in a spiritual zone of humanity, but actually in the seat of the passions. Chenu found the coherence of faith and reason in theology reinforced its anthropological integrity as it resisted the truncation of the 'science' of theology.

> La théologie est ainsi le plus beau fruit d'une confiance audacieuse dans la cohérence de la foi et de la raison, cohérence par l'intérieur, et non pas seulement accord externe par

---

126. Chenu attributed an anthropological significance to Aquinas' historical option: 'il s'en tient, pour déterminer le motif de l'incarnation, à l'histoire contingente du Christ rédempteur du péché, et résiste à la tentation de situer un Homme-Dieu au sommet de l'ordre du monde idéalement achevé.' ['To determine the reason for the Incarnation, he holds to the contingent history of Christ the redeemer of sins, and resists the temptation to locate a God-Man at the summit of the order of an ideally completed world.'] Augustine is uncharacteristically cast positively by Chenu: 'Ce fut la grandeur de la théologie de saint Augustin, et ce demeure son irrépressible séduction, de rester exclusivement centrée sur l'histoire de l'homme et de son péché, sur les imprévisibles histoires de l'amour gratuit de Dieu. Non point une métaphysique sacrée, mais une *Cité de Dieu* et des *Confessions*.' ['The grandeur of St Augustine's theology, which remains its irrepressible appeal, is remaining exclusively centred on the history of humanity and its sins, and on the unforeseeable stories of God's gratuitous love. This is no sacred metaphysics, but a *City of God* and *Confessions*.'] 'Position', 129–30.

juxtaposition de deux vérités. Cette confiance est audacieuse
parce qu'elle est fondée dans la structure même de la foi, de
la vertu «théologale» habilitant l'homme à entrer dans la
connaissance de Dieu. C'est donc la foi qui est audacieuse, et
non pas d'abord la raison.[127]
[Thus theology is the most beautiful fruit of a bold confidence
in the coherence of faith and reason, coherence through
the interior, not solely an external agreement through the
juxtaposition of two truths. This confidence is bold because
it is founded in the very structure of faith, of the 'theologal'
virtue which empowers man to enter into the knowledge of
God. It is thus faith which is bold, not reason.]

This amounted to a prolegomenon for his theological anthropology: 'la foi est lumière divine *dans* une intelligence humaine. Elle est
possédée par l'homme, et l'homme pense par elle.' ['faith is the divine
light *in* a human understanding. It is possessed by the person, and the
person thinks through it.'][128]
    While registering the danger of the reduction to either anthro-
pocentrism or theocentrism, Chenu refused the false dichotomy of
humanism opposed to theology as too simplistic. His use of the term
'théologal' in 'l'humanisme théologal' emphasised the divine and
human relationship, locating this humanism within the theological
order, as a *theo*-logal anthropology which speaks to humans of God.
This signalled an anthropological starting-point which is qualified
and enhanced by its relationship to its divine object: 'la vie théologale,
c'est-à-dire de la vie divine en nous participée, selon la triple et
unique puissance de la foi, de l'espérance, de la charité.'['theological
life, that is, the divine life in which we participate, according to the
triple and unique power of faith, hope, and charity'][129] In a sweep
through the historical drama of two renaissances, Chenu juxtaposed
'le haut équilibre spirituel' ['high spiritual equilibrium'] of Aquinas'
response to the Aristotelian humanism of his time, to the inability
of theology to correlate critically with subsequent revolutions in
human thought. Unlike the invention and critical openness of Aquinas' 'theological humanism', humanism was dismissed perfunctorily

127. 'Position', 131.
128. 'Position', 134.
129. *St Thomas d'Aquin et la théologie*, 54.

as error. In contrast, the history of the failure of 'humanist theology' demonstrated to Chenu the limitations of a too apologetic and defensive 'formalism', divorced from the 'realism' of faith. Yet he conceded that this attempt at dialogue with humanism did save Catholic doctrine from the anti-humanist challenges of Lutheranism. Chenu insisted that this 'humanist theology' was at least more theological in its refutation of the reformers than that provided against Erasmus by the Cologne Dominicans; he even praised its rich if severe spirituality, as represented by St Francis de Sales. He observed the dissimilar orientation and ends of each theological approach: 'la théologie humaniste procéda exactement à l'inverse d'un humanisme théologale.' ['humanist theology proceeds in exactly the opposite way to a theological humanism'.][130] In contrast, the 'theological humanism' of Aquinas disclosed the coherence of reason and faith within the mystery of that same faith, with that critical curiosity that marks all true humanism.[131] Chenu regretted the absence of another Aquinas in this history of doctrinal conflict and development.

'Position de la théologie' drew less attention from the Roman authorities than *Une École de théologie: le Saulchoir*, and yet it drastically broke with the conventions of neo-scholastic method. In it Chenu's particular version of 'la nouvelle théologie' was introduced as a profound renewal of theological method. While Lubac's *Catholicisme* and *Surnaturel* opened the central doctrines to the breadth of the Patristic and other non-Thomist sources, Chenu's contribution reformed even this methodology, turning '*le retour aux sources*' from a merely positivist retrieval into a '*ressourcement*', drawing on the traditional sources for constructing contemporary theology. Grounded in a retrieval of Thomas' teaching on faith, Chenu also stressed faith's critical orientation of both contemplation and theology. Faith and reason are united in their object, principle and end, and entwined in the necessary tension between faith and understanding, as expressed by Anselm's formula.

> C'est encore et toujours le *Fides quaerens intellectum* d'Anselme et de Thomas d'Aquin, mais saisi par une perception nouvelle de son objet: le mystère de Dieu entré en communication avec l'homme. La nouveauté est en ceci que, sans rejeter, bien sûr,

---

130. 'Position', 135.
131. 'Position', 135.

sa référence à Dieu, la foi trouve son objet dans une «histoire
sainte»[132]
[It is still and always will be Anselm's and Thomas Aquinas'
Fides quaerens intellectum, but grabbed by a new perception of
its object: the mystery of God which enters in communication
with the human person. Its novelty is that which, without of
course rejecting its reference to God, faith finds its object in a
'sacred history'.]

He paralleled the coherence between faith and reason in theology
with that of grace and nature: 'Cette exaltation de la raison dans le
travail théologique, c'est la consécration suprême de la nature dans la
grâce.'[133] Chenu expanded on this parallel of nature-grace and faith
and reason when arguing for the autonomy of the human sciences:

> Théologiens, c'est, pensons-nous, par les exigences mêmes
> de notre théologie qu'est requis un ordre propre de vérités
> rationnelles, tout comme la grace requiert une nature. La
> théologie est, au très fort sens médiévale du mot, une «sagesse»;
> mais une sagesse dont la transcendance même interdit une
> préséance *active* en vertu de laquelle elle interviendrait
> positivement dans l'établissement et la construction des
> disciplines rationnelles. Elle n'est pas au sommet des sciences,
> mais hors l'ordre du savoir, plantée qu'elle est par la foi dans
> la science de Dieu. Le théologian ne porte pas en soi une
> philosophie, une physique, une métaphysique, pas plus
> qu'une politique, une sociologie, ou une économie. Il n'y a pas
> continuité, scientifiquement parlant.[134]
> [Theologians, we think, that it is by the very demands of our
> theology that a proper order of rational truths is required, just
> as grace requires a nature. Theology, in the strongest medieval
> sense of the word, is a 'wisdom', but a wisdom whose very
> transcendence forbids an *active* precedence thanks to which
> it intervenes positively in the establishment and construction
> of the rational disciplines. It is not at the summit of the
> sciences, but outwith the order of knowledge, planted as it is
> by faith in the science of God. The theologian does not carry

---

132. Chenu, 'La théologie en procès', in *Savoir, faire, espérer: les limites de la raison*
     (Brussells: Facultés Universitaires St Louis, 1976), 691–696, (692).
133. 'Position', 134–5.
134. *Une école*, 153 [81]

a philosopher, a physicist, or a metaphysicist within himself,
any more than he does a politician, sociologist, or economist:
there is no continuity, scientifically speaking.]

The problem of the coherence of nature with grace, how to avoid the deprecation of nature engendered by excessively spiritual Augustinianism without compromising the divine gift of grace, became the key theme of *'la nouvelle théologie*. Echoing his earlier claim that Aquinas' genius lay in the conjunction of 'intuition' and 'mentalité', Chenu emphasised the importance of intuition as an expression of faith, because intuition reconciles the separated mystical and speculative forms of theology.[135]

Chenu's project of outlining the dynamic of faith in reason and theology was a development of the intellectualist theology of his teachers Gardeil and Garrigou-Lagrange. Yet it continued the critical overhaul of the method and presuppositions of 'modern scholasticism' initiated by the 'modernist crisis'. To some extent Chenu's *ressourcement* of Thomas can be read as continuous with Garrigou-Lagrange' work in returning to the sources of spiritual theology. There is some suggestion of this continuity in Chenu's shock at Garrigou-Lagrange's condemnation of *Une École* in 1937; he appears to have understood his task as adding an historical criticality to his master's Thomism, but he discovered there was no middle ground position between them.[136] His correlation of human reason and historical trends was deemed dangerous to the Church's doctrinal deposit, because it unveiled doctrine's historical development and the historical imperative to communicate the Gospel anew to each age. Chenu regretted

---

135. Chenu, 'La psychologie de la foi dans la théologie du XIIIe siècle.' (1932), 98: 'L'intuition, c'est l'ame religieuse de saint Thomas qui la fournit, dans l'expérience d'une affecteuse adhésion—infrangible et impatience à la fois—au Dieu béatifiant qui se révèle.' ['Intuition is provided by St Thomas' religious soul, in the experience of an affectionate attachment, both unbreakable and impatient, to the beatifying God who reveals himself.']

136. There is some support for this view in Garrigou-Lagrange's earlier attacks on incursions of nominalism and idealism into neo-scholastic thought, and his recovery of Thomas' teaching on 'common sense'. Yet his metaphysical commitment is clearly a different register from Chenu's. See particularly the contrast of his approach in *De Deo Uno: Commentarium in Primam Partem S. Thomae* (Paris: Cerf, 1938), 126–145, to Chenu's earlier articles on the *Prima Pars* and *sacra doctrina*.

how Aquinas' critical correlation of these was absent from theology in subsequent ages, and attributed this to an inadequate understanding of how central to Aquinas' theology was his teaching on faith and human understanding, and the anthropology this was grounded in.

> Toute la théologie de la foi, chez saint Thomas, est élaborée à partir des «conditions» du sujet humain, en même temps que sur l'absolu de sa divine vérité.[137]
> [All theology of faith, in St Thomas, is worked out from the 'conditions' of the human subject at the same time as on the absolute in his divine truth.]

This methodological article concluded with Chenu's account of 'l'humanisme théologal' and the concomitant anthropological implications of the Incarnation. He would explore this further in his manifesto *Une école de théologie: le Saulchoir*:

> *Cognita sunt in cognoscente ad modum cognoscentis*: exclure Dieu de cette loi naturelle de toute connaissance, sous prétexte qu'il est transcendant ou qu'il se révèle, ce serait céder d'avance au désordre spirituel d'une fausse mysticité. Si vraiment l'homme connaît Dieu, il le connaîtra humainement. Pas plus que la grâce en la nature, la foi n'est une lumière posée à la surface d'une raison: elle vit en elle. Et la foi n'est pas contaminée pas cette incarnation, pas plus que le Verbe n'est amoindri pour s'être fait chair. Double mystère théandrique, mieux, unique mystère, qui est le mystère même du Christ, en qui le divin et l'humain sont un: unique Personne, en laquelle la foi me plante, Fils éternel de Dieu entré dans l'histoire. Le Christ de la foi, dans le Christ de l'histoire.[138]
> [*Cognita sunt in cognoscente ad modum cognoscentis*: to exclude God from this natural law of all knowledge on the pretext that he is transcendent or that he reveals himself would be to give in in advance to the spiritual disorder of a false mysticism. If man truly knows God, he knows him humanly. No more than grace in nature, faith is not a light placed at the surface of a reason, it lives in it. And faith is not contaminate by this incarnation, any more than the Word reduced himself to become flesh. The double theandric mystery or better, the

---

137. 'Vérité et liberté dans la foi du croyant' (1959), 358.
138. *Une école de théologie*, 60–61 [136–137].

single mystery, which is the mystery of Christ himself, in whom divine and human are one: a single Person, in whom faith roots me, the eternal Son of God who entered history. The Christ of faith, in the Christ of history.]

For Chenu, it is a false mysticism that denies the role of human reason in the phenomenon of faith and thereby risks the unity of human understanding. That a dualist concept of humanity would be the result was for him a compromise of the Incarnation, for it deems humanity as incapable of bearing the mystery of Christ. His slogan, 'Si vraiment l'homme connaît Dieu, il le connaîtra humainement' ['if man truly knew God, he would know him humanly'], captured the significance for Christian anthropology of avoiding such a bifurcated understanding. Human understanding is not limited to appreciating creation only but is open to God's revelation through its very same faculties for knowing. God is known humanly, and any separation of the capacity for faith understanding from other knowledge destabilises the whole concept of what it means to be human. Chenu continued his theological investigation from this human perspective in his early ecclesiological writings, before and after his condemnation in 1937.

History, Culture, and Revelation: Marie-Dominique Chenu, OP

Thomas F O'Meara, OP

The French historian and theologian Marie-Dominique Chenu in his long life offered ideas and inspiration to theologians and historians, pastoral activists and bishops. The Dominican was an outstanding historian of the twelfth and thirteenth centuries even as he was a creative voice in the renewal of the Catholic Church in the twentieth century. His writings on Thomas Aquinas' theology in the cultural world of his time are still considered by some to be outstanding synthetic works on Aquinas written in the decades of the twentieth century, a time that produced a number of outstanding scholars on medieval thought.[1]

Thomas Aquinas and Culture

Chenu stressed that Thomas Aquinas was a product and a gift of his time, of the world around him in the thirteenth century as Europe was learning from Greek Christian and Islamic libraries and schools.

> Cultural dimensions in the course of history go beyond academic teaching. They emerge in new images and lead the religious dimension to find new mental categories and vocabularies. There were new disciplines, new sciences, particularly those treating the human person. Albert the Great, Thomas' teacher, wrote that science was far from complete: new sciences are awaiting discovery. Theology

---

1. Chenu, *La théologie comme science au XIIIe siècle* (Paris: J Vrin, 1943 [*Toward Understanding Saint Thomas* (Chicago: Regnery, 1964)]; *La Théologie au douzième siècle* (Paris: J Vrin, 1957); *Nature, Man and Society in the Twelfth Century* (Chicago: University of Chicago Press, 1968).

appears as a historical dimension of the life of the church at
the same time as the life of the church enters into the breadth
of theology.[2]

In the concluding decades of the twelfth century the arts, sciences, and
theological disciplines were full of promise. The forms of that age in the
arts—moving from Notre Dame to the Sainte-Chapelle—correspond
to the world of Albert and Aquinas. Before the pictorial creations of
colored glass or in the lecture halls of the university, a person might feel
at home among similar ways of expression. Aquinas lived in the worlds
of the new universities and of the Gothic culture around him. 'Analyz-
ing the historical and social conditions of Aquinas' work is a very good
way of observing the truth of his teaching in relationship to its place in
civilization and its role in the course of theological development.'[3]

Chenu was both historian and theologian. 'History in theology lies
at the inner reality of theology itself.'[4] History could mean the location
of Greek and Arabic philosophies in Christian thinking or it could
mean the appearance, flourishing, and decline of the creative forms
of an age. Although the *Summa theologiae* was commented on exten-
sively century after century, Chenu was a central figure in disclosing
its organizational structure, its patterns. A basic thought-form joined
the three large parts: it was methodological, pedagogical, theological, and aesthetic. This was not the building blocks of an Aristotelian
science but a Neoplatonic procession outwards of beings from a first
principle and their subsequent movement toward fulfillment in that
same source.[5] Every being and action, of nature and grace, with their
production and destiny, could be located and illumined in the lines of
the processes God has set in motion. The *telos*, the attracting goal in
the future, however, should not be conceived as a 'return', a backward
move. The process seeks its fulfillment (not an end) going forward. It
is best to imagine the course of the *Summa theologiae* not as a circular
return but as an upward spiral. Creation becomes history.

---

2. Chenu, 'An Innovator in a New World', Thomas O'Meara, editor, *Exploring
    Thomas Aquinas. Essays and Sermons* (Chicago: New Priory Press, 2017), 17.
3. Chenu, 'Preface', Henri Petitot, *Life and Spirit of Thomas Aquinas* (Chicago:
    Priory Press, 1966), 6.
4. Chenu, 'Avant-propos', *La théologie au douzième siècle*, 14.
5. Aquinas, *In I Sent*, d. 14, q. 2, a. 2.

The pattern is Christian as well as Neoplatonic. Revelation teaches that along with a universe of beings there is a history of a special presence of God, grace, missions of the divine Word and Spirit to intelligent creatures. The totality of the divine work, reaching a climax in the human being, goes on to its source for biological existence and shared divine life. The movement outward of beings through their forms and toward their goals includes even God in a Trinity of active persons, giving and receiving eternally. Thomas borrowed 'from the grandiose Neoplatonic vision of the universe conceived in terms of an emanation and a return that defines the dynamics of each creature participating in the divine realm. Thomas uses this schema to design the structure for his *Summa theologiae* within which salvation history, the incarnation of Christ included, enters into this predestined plan of divine Love's expansion'.[6] Drawn from the Greek fathers recently rediscovered in the cultural world of the twelfth and thirteenth century, this dynamic thread is trinitarian and incarnational.[7] For all things God is the term of their procession, return, fulfillment—in their different ways.

Chenu noticed further sub-patterns, Christian or philosophical themes and thought-forms, biblical and patristic sources. 'I was shocked by the rigid and systematic way in which the Aristotelian structures present in the text were commented upon in detail, while the sap of evangelical and patristic spirituality supplying life to these otherwise dead branches was ignored or glossed over.'[8] For instance, in the *Summa theologiae* the Christology drew from Greek patristic works, while sin took ideas and motifs from Augustine. Exemplary causality appeared in the theology of creation as well as in that of sacrament. There are different kinds of faith, while justice might be developed from Roman legal documents or from the Hebrew scriptures.

---

6. Chenu, *Aquinas and His Role in Theology* (Collegeville: Liturgical Press, 2002) 98.
7. See Aquinas, *Compendium of Theology* (St Louis: Herder, 1948); see O Pesch, 'Um den Plan der *Summa theologiae* des hl. Thomas von Aquin', K Bernath, editor, *Thomas von Aquin* 1 (Darmstadt: Wissenschaftliche Buchgesellschaft, 1978), 128ff; A Patfoort, 'L'unité de la Ia Pars et le mouvement interne de la *Somme théologique* de s. Thomas d'Aquin', in *Revue des sciences philosophiques et théologiques*, 47 (1963): 514–526.
8. Chenu, *Toward Understanding*, 309.

Like other French scholars of the time Chenu saw parallels between Gothic art and medieval theology. Louis Grodecki writes: 'There was contact between the theologians and the architects. Pierre de Montreuil, the chief of construction of the Sainte-Chapelle, according to an ancient tradition was described on his funeral stone as a Professor of Masonry.[9] Erwin Panofsky observed that the then popular form of the *summa*—in philosophy, theology, law, and history—is marked by drawing together several areas and linking them through connecting themes, something seen in the new churches' images.[10] In the new churches two aspects step forth: structure joined to appearance, and the use of light. If the expansion of stained glass came from Arab technology and Aristotelian realism, the theology behind it was that Neoplatonism whose sources were in the libraries of the royal abbey of St Denis or of the Parisian intellectual center of the Abbey of St Victor. Chenu wrote that the patterns of ideas, 'the internal relationship of objects and themes under consideration', suggests the 'comparison between *summa*s and cathedrals—both significant products of medieval civilization'.[11] Color and distinction serve presence and spirit.

To enter a Gothic church is to encounter incarnation: spirit in a geometry of stone, color in glass, and light in air. All of this directs light down into the church, inspiring the human spirit to go upwards and outwards. The medieval theologian wrote: 'Grace is caused in people by the presence of the divinity just as light is caused in the atmosphere by the presence of the sun.'[12] Divine light active in

---

9. Louis Grodecki, *La Sainte-Chapelle* (Paris: Éditions de la Caisse Nationale des Monuments Historiques et des Sites, 1975), 4.

10. See Erwin Panofsky, *Gothic Architecture and Scholasticism* (New York: Meridian Books, 1957), 29ff. 'Is Panofsky's problematic about a possible connection between gothic architecture and scholasticism illegitimate? Not at all, for certainly a century like the unusual thirteenth raises the issue of the inner dependence and mutual relationships of so many cultural streams and innovations' (A Speer, 'Thomas von Aquin und die Kunst', in *Archiv fur Kulturgeschichte*, 72 [1990]: 343); see GA Zinn, Jr, 'Suger, Theology, and the Pseudo-Dionysian Tradition', in *Abbot Suger and Saint-Denis: A Symposium* (New York: Metropolitan Museum of Art, 1986), 33ff.

11. Chenu, *Aquinas and His Role in Theology*, 137; see Otto von Simson, *The Origins of Gothic Architecture and the Medieval Concept of Order* (New York: Harper and Row, 1962).

12. *Summa theologiae* III, q. 7, a. 12. Chenu, *Toward Understanding*, 35.

humans is displayed by figures and events, usually from the biblical narratives. These pictures of color and light lead the believer in the church to move upward spiritually to the divine Source. A stone and glass structure holding and channeling light has parallels with Aquinas' theology of divine presence enhancing the human psychology. The pictures present the dynamic activity of God, revelation teaching people in their concrete world and grace assisting their lives.

Chenu and His Times

Born of enlightenment science, idealism's systems, and existentialist novels culture had focused attention on the active self and its temporality. Modern thought changed the meaning of the term 'world'.[13] A world was not just unfettered nature or a monarchical state: it was the existence and milieu around an independent person. History was not merely a chronological background but time penetrating everything. Around 1800, Friedrich Schlegel said that the new modernity revolved around three things: the structures of the knowing self, freedom, and history. The self-fashions, interprets, and expands the reality it knows, making it into its world. Walter Kasper writes: 'European thought is determined by two basic possibilities. The first is a thinking proceeding from being, essence, nature, fact; the second begins with freedom understood as an activity disclosing the world.'[14] Through natural science, styles of art, psychology, and religion the forms of the human spirit influence how people think.

After 1790, the Roman Catholic Church saw itself threatened by the modern: analytic psychology, democratic society, social history, and human evolution. Nonetheless, in the first half of the nineteenth century the ideas of Friedrich Schelling, G W F Hegel, and others influenced Catholic theologians like Johann Adam Möhler and Franz

---

13. Martin Heidegger wrote: 'World is not the mere collection of things at hand that are either calculable or not; known or unknown. World is never an object that just stands before to be looked at . . . World is always the non-objectifiable before which we stand' (Heidegger, *Der Ursprung des Kunstwerkes* [Stuttgart: Reclam, 1960], 44, 56).

14. Kasper, 'Verständnis der Geschichte in der Theologie', in *Theologie im Wandel* (Munich: Wewel, 1967), 112; see the proceedings of the symposium touching on Chenu and cultural periods: *Marie-Dominique Chenu. Moyen-âge et modernité* (Paris: Centre d'études du Saulchoir, 1997).

von Baader. They restored some Pauline and patristic perspectives of what it means to be the Christian church, a charismatic and ministerial organism passing through cultural periods.[15] After each of the two World Wars, Catholic thinkers like French Dominicans and German Jesuits began to pursue a further dialogue with modern thought ranging from economics to sculpture. In the 1950s ecumenism, Bible study groups, sacramental preparation, modern mosaics in churches, and liturgical renewal emerged, struggling to escape the tight control of Vatican bureaucrats.

When the young Chenu entered the Dominicans, church authority was working to retain the monoform ideology of restored scholasticism.[16] The church needed only one: Latin, Baroque, neo-scholastic. In the 1940s, seeing that a great effort was needed to vitalize the church in Europe, Cardinal Emmanuel Suhard of Paris published pastoral letters on the problematical condition of the Church in France. In *La France, Pays de Mission?* he dared to call France 'a missionary country'.[17] Laity and clergy joined Suhard in starting new organizations. Both the impotency of the old parish structure and the lack of success of the Catholic Action movement hesitantly sponsored by Rome in the 1920s called for new directions. The theologians of the 1940s and 1950s were not reclusive seminary professors or agents of the magisterium but theologians of depth, applicants of the New Testament to culture. Through writings and evening seminars Chenu sought to meet the changing times of French society. What were they saying to the church about expressing the Gospel and forming a community of movements? He worked with Jeunesse Ouvrière Chrétienne (the 'Jocists') as well as with the leadership of Mission de France and Mission de Paris. Days involved demonstrations for

---

15. O'Meara, 'Beyond "Hierarchology": Johann Adam Möhler and Yves Congar', in Donald J Dietrich, Michael J Himes, editors, *The Legacy of the Tübingen School: The Relevance of Nineteenth-Century Theology for the Twenty-First Century* (New York: Crossroad, 1997), 173–191.

16. Otto Pesch described these neo-Thomisms as keeping Thomas Aquinas 'under house arrest' (*Thomas von Aquin. Grenze und Grösse mittelalterlicher Theologie* [Mainz: Matthias-Grünewald, 1989], 27).

17. Henri Godin, Yves David, *France, Pays de Mission?* (Paris: Éditions de l'abeille, 1943). On the rise of progressive movements in Paris, many allied to the Dominicans, see Yvon Tranvouez, *Catholiques et Communistes. La crise du progressisme Chrétien, 1950–1955* (Paris: Cerf, 2000).

peace, while evenings were spent at union meetings making friends and talking theology with fellow activists.

Chenu saw the *Summa theologiae* as a source for new ideas and ministerial movements. Both personal spirituality and social movements are aided by Aquinas' pneumatology. His 'objective spirituality' (more than 'an interior life') of psychological powers and dynamics should replace the cloistered introspection of an elite group: it would highlight the 'Gospel in contrast to the pastoral pietism and the pious moralizing of previous spiritual writers'.[18] All the baptised compose the church; all are being vivified by the Spirit; all are called to ministries new and old. 'A human being is a composite of body and soul, and made up of various members. The Catholic Church is like this, too. It is one body with many members who are different. The 'soul' that gives life to this body is the Holy Spirit.'[19] Grace drawing the human person to active life in the reign of God—this is Aquinas' often cited basic principle. 'Grace allows nature to be free to be itself and also leads it on to its completion in both communities and individuals, in both action and contemplation.'[20] God is speaking to me as a human being, and I am going to undertake a dialogue with God as a human being. 'Faith will never be something extrinsic introduced into my living organism or like a list of dead propositions in my spirit. Rather it is a force within me, one of dynamic intelligence.'[21] In it the powers of human psychology and the plan of divine love come into play. Belief, awe, reflection—all the aspects of theology—will arise out of a meeting of grace with human experience.

Grace was not only psychological but social. 'Charity is political in its own special way; this goes beyond considerations of people helping each other. The social and political demands of public order are not dissolved by the presence of charity.'[22] Forms of socialism are forms of humanism struggling to vitalize terrestrial society. The human per-

---

18. Chenu, *Aquinas and His Role in Theology*, 43. Janette Gray called Chenu's writings 'a Socio-Political Christian Anthropology' (*M-D Chenu's Christian Anthropology: Nature and Grace in Society and Church* [Hindmarsh, South Australia: ATF Theology, 2019]) Chapter six.

19. Aquinas, *Commentary on the Creed*, a 9.

20. Chenu, *Aquinas and His Role in Theology*, 11.

21. Chenu, *Aquinas and His Role in Theology*, 23.

22. Chenu, *Aquinas and His Role in Theology*, 112; *La doctrine sociale de l'Église comme idéologie* (Paris: Cerf, 1979).

son has significant causal powers. 'On account of the abundance of his goodness (and not at all as a defect in power) God communicates to creatures the dignity of causality.'[23] Church and society unfold God's subtle assistance in human beings working to attain justice and grace. To give finite active beings their due does not diminish God but recognizes his power. In terms of free beings, Chenu concluded, 'God is equally the source and master of the variety in their being, in their contingency and necessity, in their determined nature and freedom. He gives to each their own special reality.'[24]

Surprisingly Chenu was active in the Christian dialogue with the Arabic world. He helped establish after 1938 the Dominican Institute in Cairo. He encouraged two of his students at Le Saulchoir in the 1930s to meet scholars in Paris knowledgeable in the mysticism and culture of Islam. Georges Anawati and Jacques Jomier were founding members of the Institute and had an extraordinary influence for decades in that world.[25]

Conflicts

In 1941, a Dominican priest Jacques Loew began an unusual form of ministry: he got a job working on the docks at the port of Marseille, France. He could little imagine the reverberations soon to be created by a Catholic priest finding a job, earning a wage, and living in a poor apartment house. Paris and Marseille witnessed a new kind of priest. The first priest-workers lived alone or, if they were religious, in groups of two or three. They were, however, catalysts in developing communities of religious and laity, and soon such groups active in labor and peace movements were at work from Lyons to Belgium. By 1953 there were ninety priest-workers. They could hardly avoid the strong presence of the Communist Party, and some joined Communist led unions rather than try to work with the less effective Catho-

---

23. *Summa theologiae* I, q. 22, a. 3.
24. Chenu, *Aquinas and His Role in Theology*, 89.
25. Georges C Anawati, 'Le Père Chenu et l'Institut dominicain d'Études orientales du Caire', C Geffré, editor, *L'Hommage différé au Père Chenu* (Paris: Cerf, 1990), 63–67; Dennis Halft, 'Towards a New Perception of Islam: The Influence of Marie-Dominique Chenu's Theology of Incarnation on Christian-Muslim Relations', in Michael Attridge *et al*, editors, *The Promise of Renewal. Dominicans and Vatican II* (Adelaide: ATF Theology, 2017), 227–257.

lic ones. A few of the priest-workers left the priesthood, and a few became dedicated Marxists.[26]

While not neglecting the world of medieval theology, Chenu composed theological position papers for new urban ministries. He wrote articles and books on a theology of work. That led to the medieval scholar becoming a theological adviser to the priest-workers.[27] In February, 1954, he published a controversial article on 'The Priesthood of the Worker Priests'. If the priesthood means clerical clothes, breviary, and a private silent Mass, then the priest workers are a different kind of a priest. 'We do not accept that the priesthood is limited to sacramental and cultic functions. Those things presuppose witnessing to the faith as the first act of the church of Christians.'[28] Community, liturgy, and service belong together. Today there are many ways to give searching groups the word of God and the body of Christ. 'The movement of the priest-workers is the most important religious movement since the French Revolution.'[29]

In October, 1953, Giuseppe Cardinal Pizzardo, director of the Vatican's Holy Office (formerly the Inquisition) wrote to the head of the Dominicans Emmanuel Suarez: 'You know well the new ideas and tendencies, not only exaggerated but even erroneous, that are developing in the realms of theology, canon law, and society, ideas finding a considerable resonance in certain religious orders . . . so-called theologians 'with brilliant phrases and generalizations' teach

---

26. Catherine Masson 'Ruptures et renouveaux: la question des prêtres-ouvriers (1953–1965)', in *Mélanges de science religieuse*, 61 (2004): 79.

27. See O'Meara, 'Jacques Loewe: Ministry on the Docks', in Thomas O'Meara, Paul Philibert, editors, *Scanning the Signs of the Times. French Dominicans in the Twentieth Century* (Adelaide: ATF Theolpgy, 2013), 81–96; Oscar Cole-Arnal, 'From the Docks of Marseille to Vatican II: The Pivotal Role of the Dominican Worker-Priests (1942–1965)', in Attridge, *et al*, editors, *The Promise of Renewal. Dominicans and Vatican II*, 307–320.

28. Ulrich Engel, 'Bürgerliche Priester—proletarische Priester. Ein Lehrstück aus der Konfliktgeschichte zwischen Kirche und Arbeiterschaft', *Gott der Menschen. Wegmarken dominikanischer Theologie* (Mainz: Matthias-Grünewald, 2010), 142.

29. François Leprieur, *Quand Rome condamne. Dominicains et prêtres-ouvriers* (Paris: Plon/Cerf, 1989), 765. 'Is it not surprising to find Père Chenu at the founding session of the Mission de Paris at the end of 1943 among the priests of *Action populaire*? Even more, in terms of ideas Chenu became one of the most faithful and helpful companions of the *Mission de Paris* on its journey' (Leprieur, *Quand Rome condamne*, 24).

falsehood.'[30] Suarez flew to Paris and removed from office the three French provincials and the provincial directors of studies. Some professors of theology were forbidden to teach, and some found the Vatican controlling what they could publish. The Roman action was in strong opposition to the Dominican tradition of democracy in the selection of superiors. Chenu's student Yves Congar wrote: 'There are people who accuse us of modernism. That's unjust and libelous. They have no sense of history.'[31]

Because Chenu supported the priest worker movement personally and intellectually the Roman measures against those priests and sisters had personal consequences for him.[32] He was not only removed from the school he directed, Le Saulchoir, but banned from lecturing and publishing. No doubt he recalled Aquinas' view of theological autocracy in the thirteenth century: 'There are actually people who presume that their judgment is so reliable that they can measure by their own understanding the nature of anything. They think that however they judge it is true, and whatever they judge to be false must be wrong.'[33] Chenu was rehabilitated by becoming a consulting theologian at Vatican II. He was not an official adviser but a personal *peritus* to an African bishop who had been his student at Le Saulchoir. In the opening months of the Council he advocated producing a message to all peoples about the hopes of that assembly. This would become *Gaudium et Spes.*[34]

---

30. Cited in Leprieur, *Quand Rome condamne,* 42–45; see Thomas O'Meara, 'Raid on the Dominicans: The Repression of 1954', in *America* 170 (1994): 8–16.

31. Jean-M Le Guillou, 'Yves Congar', H Vorgrimler, Robert vander Gucht, editors, *Bilanz der Theologie im 20 Jh,* 4 *Bahnbrechende Theologen* (Freiburg: Herder, 1970), 10. 'I have to struggle: both for my liberty, my honour and also within myself, against the abominable and non-Christian den of thieves that is the Roman Inquisition' (Congar, *Journal of a Theologian (1946-1958)* [Adelaide: ATF Theology, 2013], 252); see Johannes Bunnenberg, 'In den Fängen des Hl. Offiziums. "Die düsteren Jahre" des Dominikaners Yves Congar', in *Wort und Antwort,* 44 (2003): 19–24.

32. See Leprieur, *Quand Rome condamne,* 100f.

33. Aquinas, *Summa contra Gentiles* I, 5. 'Persons whose opinions we accept as well as those whose ideas we reject—both groups are applying themselves to the search for truth. Both are collaborators with us in our own search' (*Commentary on the Metaphysics,* 12, 9).

34. M Quisinsky, *Geschichtlicher Glaube in einer geschichtlichen Welt. Der Beitrag von M.-D. Chenu, Y. Congar und H.-M Féret zum II. Vaticanum* (Münster: Lit, 2007), 31–171; see his journal of the conciliar period, M-D Chenu, *Vatican II Notebook* (Adelaide: ATF Theology, 2015).

At Work for 'The New'

Chenu's influence on the Dominican faculty of Le Saulchoir is obvious, and his contact with Yves Congar is well known. Through decades there were others influenced like Edward Schillebeeckx;[35] a pioneer of religious education, Henri-Marie Féret; Louis Charlier who brought the historical study of Aquinas to the University of Leuven; and the American advocate of creation-centered spirituality, Matthew Fox.[36]

Chenu liked to refer to a passage about Aquinas written by William of Tocco, a student at the University of Naples from 1272 to 1274 and Aquinas' biographer: 'To hear him teach was to be in contact with a new doctrine supported by new argumentation. One could not doubt that God by touching him with a new light and with a newness of inspiration led him to teach, from the beginning of his professorship, openly and directly, in word and in writing, new views.'[37] Chenu noticed how often the word '*novus*' appeared.

> This must be an intentional repetition . . . Friar Thomas, stimulated by the cultural changes of his time, found in them an impetus to give newness to teaching. Content and method, spirit and technique, principles and conclusion, style and inspiration—all the elements of this lofty knowledge of God came together to manifest a new kind of theology. The encounter of faith with a new culture was the reason and the motivation for this theology.[38]

Different cultural ages stimulate different modes of incarnation. Seven hundred years later the Spirit was inspiring Christians to draw

---

35. Schillebeeckx's doctoral dissertation from Le Saulchoir was *L'économie sacramentelle du salut: réflexion théologique sur la doctrine sacramentaire de saint Thomas, à la lumière de la tradition et de la problématique sacramentelle contemporaine* (Fribourg: Academia, 2004); see 'In memory of Marie-Dominique (Marcel) Chenu, OP (January 7, 1895- February 11, 1990)', Schillebeeckx, *I Am a Happy Theologian. Conversations with Francesco Strazzari* (London: SCM, 1994); *Un théologien en liberté. Jacques Duquesne interroge le Père Chenu* (Paris: Le Centurion, 1975).
36. Fox, *Confessions. The Making of a Post-Denominational Priest* (San Francisco: HarperSanFrancisco, 1996).
37. William of Tocco, *Ystoria sancti Thomae de Aquino* (Toronto: Pontifical Institute of Medieval Studies, 1996), 121–122.
38. Chenu, 'An Innovator in a New World', Thomas O'Meara, editor, *Exploring Thomas Aquinas* 1f.

from the Gospel what Chenu saw as new incarnations. 'For the incarnation of God of which the newness of Christianity is both the sign and the mystery, does not occur once and for all in a corner of Judea. It lasts on and on; it exists always; it exists everywhere.'[39] In an interview on the occasion of his eightieth birthday Chenu emphasised the important of seeing a continuing incarnation. Incarnation describes a deep and guided interplay of the divine and the human. There are different kinds of incarnation in faith, liturgy, and church. Christophe Potworowski writes: 'Chenu's commitment to the concreteness of history—or, better, to the historicity of human knowing—is most clearly expressed in his view of theology as a reading of the signs of the times.'[40] This reading leads to openness, activity, and inculturation.

Chenu was a happy extrovert. When he met a visitor to the Priory of St. Jacques where he lived in Paris, a crossroads for Dominicans from around the world, he welcomed the friar at once, and asked about where he worked and what he did. Distant and new provinces and schools were congratulated. In his nineties, he praised each person's ministry and writings as signs of hope for the Order and the church. His Dominican brothers observed of him, 'He prays every day to stay alive and keep working'. He died aged 95 in 1990.

---

39. Chenu, *La Parole de Dieu* II (Paris: Cerf, 1964), 9.
40. Potworowski, *Contemplation and Incarnation. The Theology of Marie-Dominique Chenu* (Montreal: McGIll-Queen's University Press, 2001), xv.; see Dennis Halft, 'Towards a New Perception of Islam: The Influence of Marie-Dominique Chenu's Theology of Incarnation on Christian-Muslim relations', in Attridge, *et al*, editors, *The Promise of Renewal. Dominicans and Vatican II*, 227–241.

InterfaceTheology 7/2 2021

Catholic Action and the Mystical Body

Marie-Dominique Chenu, OP

When we study Christian doctrine and try to define its fundamental concepts and internal construction, we would make a great mistake if we considered only the speculative formulae and explanations which we find in the text-books. Of course we have there the code of dogma in which the authentic teaching of revelation is faithfully and integrally preserved; for, as the theologians say, these are the '*loci*' which, according to their quality, contain truth and certitude. Nevertheless they must be considered in the actual *milieu* which is proposed to our faith, that is the living Church of today where these truths find their natural surroundings, their context and their synthetic sense—in the Church, the shelter and the dwelling-place of the Holy Spirit. To do this is not to add any new elements to these doctrines, but merely consists in considering them, all of them, in their proper light and natural 'habitat'.

But, if we look at the Christendom of to-day, with its aspirations, its activities and its attainments, we are struck by two facts which are of great moment, two facts which are the expression of the most traditional teaching but which, in the Church of our time, have renewed the importance and the application of these traditional doctrines. The first of these facts is external and concerns the organisation of the Church, of its apostolate: it is the development of Catholic Action. The second is internal and is manifested by the fervour of souls: it is the renewal of the doctrine of and of devotion to the Mystical Body of Christ.

These two *facts*: the theological renaissance of the Pauline doctrine of the Mystical Body, and the incessant invitation to Catholic Action of our Holy Father, would seem to have, in the life of the Church, an intimate though rather hidden connection. Their expansion, both internally and externally, cannot be fortuitous. We believe that they are intertwined, and consequently that we can increase our understanding of each of them by a consideration of their interdependence. We would go further and say that neither the definition of Catholic Action, nor its structure, nor its elements, nor its spirit is really intelligible except in terms of that Communion of Saints which we profess in the Creed. This we have neglected because we have not yet realised its importance, both spiritual and apostolic. It is precisely the work of theologians to work out these internal connections which manifest the compactness of revealed truth.

Canon Cardijn, the founder of the JOC [Young Christian Workers] (the movement which Pope Pius XI has called *ipsa germaha forma actionis catholicae*), tells the story of how he went one day to visit a well-known Catholic Action theorist, the author of many and weighty tomes on this subject. 'Before going to see this learned man', says Canon Cardijn not without humour, 'I practically knew what the J.O.C. was; after two hours' conversation I certainly did not know any longer'. The sight of, Christendom at work, under the inspiration and the direction of the Magisterium, is an indispensable support and the luminous soul of a theological analysis:

Human Society

Even the briefest of glances at the modern world will convince us of a characteristic which is found universally and in all its elements; the least human act like the slightest reality is bound up in a social order which rules it and which penetrates it to its every part. I cannot make the smallest commercial transaction, draw the lowest salary, make the most insignificant contract or agreement, without finding that I am encircled—and upheld—by those economic, social, juridical and political solidarities which, even before I decided to act, make up the subject of my agreement, my work or my business. From one end of the world to the other these things cross and re-cross, making an ever more complicated and complicating network; today, without my thinking of it, my income may be increased due to a rise on Wall Street; tomorrow my small business may go bankrupt because of cutthroat competition from the dictatorial industrialism of Japan. And so on, all over world, in every sphere of human activity. Social life enfolds me intimately and without cease.

It is many centuries since Aristotle declared that man is a social being. Everything which is in man is born, grows, flourishes—and dies—in and through society.

This is a 'law of nature' (and we know what Aristotle meant by that); it is inevitable, being without restriction and without exception. Man, being a moral and religious person, stands out from his living surroundings, and because of his soul which is always free he can avoid all abuse of power in society. And, in fact, he must do this, since the communitarian regime in any stage of development or under any form exists to serve the autonomous vocation and destiny of the human person. But man's inviolable personality is rooted in society, and finds therein strength, nourishment and help even when it is oppressed. Man cannot live and grow, bodily, intellectually and culturally except in society.[1]

This ancient doctrine was taught and practised, under various forms, in the Middle Ages, but was crushed by liberal individualism; and even the most Christian of men were ill at ease in trying to assess the human value of the tremendous 'socialisation' which was ushered in with the twentieth century. Even where there appears to be personal activity, where men seem to administer their goods personally, there is always a hidden network of strength and of servitude which guarantees, yet regulates, their use. The common good penetrates to the heart of even the most secret transaction, it is part and parcel of social and economic reality. No one is more conscious of this than the lawyer who sees the civil code continually restricted by the encroachments of community rights, and who notes the introduction of a social element in even the most personal negotiation. The totalitarian states, whether of the Right or of the Left, find here that part of the truth which makes their ideas the most seductive and dangerous.

Thus the activities of the humblest labourer, like that of the most powerful magnate, is more than ever bound up, by circles which stretch indefinitely, in the many rhythms of society. Work, business, industry, thrift, teaching, even the employment of leisure, are no longer, can no longer, be done, except in social groups, soon them-

---

1. Leo XIII makes this doctrine his own: 'Man is born to live in society; alone he can neither procure what is necessary or useful for life, nor acquire perfection of mind and heart. Therefore has Providence made him to join with his fellows, in domestic and civil society, the only one capable of giving him what is necessary for the perfection of his being.' [Editors note: source not given by the author.]

selves linked together in an organism which grows unceasingly. Even though this movement towards socialisation has been more obvious, and indeed more cruel, in economic structures both of capital and labour, it is none the less true of the whole field of human enterprise and activity. There are possible inconveniences attached to it—some of them bid fair to be dangers—but on the whole one cannot deny the immense benefits of the socialisation of human resources and activity. There may be the danger of a terrible constraint, but it is only in proportion to the growth of wealth. Not only would it be vain to fulminate against 'social progress', but it would be an error against the *natural* law of human perfection. For it cannot be denied that human, perfection is to be gained socially, and that the person finds a greater and more steady opportunity of progress in a more general socialisation of material and spiritual wealth.

The Christian Community

This law of nature can also be stated in terms of the law of grace. That which for the philosopher is the behaviour of a man is for the theologian the behaviour of a Christian. The moment, that anything, anything at all, which is of human value exists it is also the substance of Christian values, because everything which is human has been redeemed by Christ and is saved in Christ. Thus all the social values of mankind ought to enter, like individual values, into the Christian life. The individual and the social are in fact the two; facets of one and the same perfection.

In reality, it is in society that God saves man, not individually but in the grace of Christ in Whom all are one, according to the magnificent words of the 'priestly prayer' (St John, xv 17). This is the law of the Incarnation: He has not merely come in the flesh of the Word, but He is both God and head of humanity. This is accomplished in a 'Communion'; it is attained in the Mystical Body.

The law of nature can be stated in terms of the law of grace. A Christian cannot sanctify himself by a mystical escape from the social order. He cannot even accept the idea that society should be sanctified, as it were, on the rebound in the sense that if all the members are holy the collectivity will be holy. In the same way that persons can only gain perfection in and through society, so a Christian can only win perfection by plunging himself more and more deeply into the

Christian communion. Brotherly love is consubstantial with the love of God.

So we cannot at all accept a disjunction between the social and the individual, where the person would sanctify himself and the society would remain the external matter of sanctity. Indeed, speaking absolutely, would this even be possible? In any case this is not the economy wished by God, for His is the economy of the Incarnation. It is because it has accepted this disjunction that a certain part of the Christian world has earned the violent criticism of Marx. A misunderstanding of the social, of its grandeur as of its importance, has characterised quite a period of Christian thought and practice—I mean that in certain parts, which always exist, there has been side by side with obscurantism and falling away, a lack of eminent witnesses to this Christian law. To-day the revival of the doctrine of the Mystical Body, and the magnificent fervour which it arouses even in the souls of the most simple, makes us conscious of that worldly negligence which left it like a talent buried in the ground and bearing no fruit.

Dialectical materialism had an easy task against this distinguished form of spirituality, against this 'ideology' which ignored material things and the social consequences of which it is the economic support, leaving them to their earthy weight and to the frightful play of their oppression. 'It is easy to be a saint so long as one gives up being human', wrote Karl Marx. It was a false and an empty sanctity that would not recognise the fundamental conditions of human nature. But the Christian does recognise them, and this not by concession, but because he knows that his God, Christ become man, accepted them and consecrated them not merely by the fact of the Incarnation but in the restored order, the order of the Mystical Body, which is the Incarnation continued.

When Pius XI wishes to give an example of Catholic Action he points to the JOC: the authentic realisation among the workers of 'the participation of the laity in the hierarchic apostolate of the Church But it is precisely in the JOC, in the simple souls of the young Christian workers', that we notice the greatest renewal of faith and of fervour through the doctrine of the Mystical Body. This is a very significant connection which illustrates quite well the truth that Catholic Action has its foundation, its deepest reason, in the brotherly communion of the Mystical Body.

Once we admit that God became incarnate that He might divinise man, we must say, too, that He took *all* that was in man, from the highest to the lowest. If there was anything left out, escaping from this, it would not be divinised, it would not be redeemed. That is the rule of the divine life thus inaugurated on earth. There is a false reverence in the Docetism which wishes to guard the transcendence of God and so limits the humanisation of the Word. The Word was made flesh; they are the words of Saint John, categorical and made heavy with the weight of all mankind.

If such is the law of the Incarnation for Christ, so, too, is it the law of the incarnation of the divine life throughout centuries in the Church of Christ. The whole man, all his resources and his works, is taken up by grace. The divine life is not infused into our life by an elimination of its human content, nor by a reduction of its native structure, but by a totalitarian elevation to the supernatural plane. Whatever remained outside this sanctification would be lost, not merely in a negative way by not being won back, but positively, for it is corruptive waste, it is the mass which has been left untouched by the yeast. Here again we must not give in to that reverence which will not face reality and which refuses to see in the Church the Body of Christ incarnated, incorporated in humanity.

In the first place this concerns, quite evidently, the constitutive resources of man, those which condition his being and his progress—and thus that social structure of man in which alone he can acquire his perfection. The law of nature becomes the law of grace.

But, as we have remarked, during the past century this law of nature with an ever accelerated rhythm is playing a greater part in the economic, social and political life of man; a great yet a tragic spectacle, wherein the very perversions of this social life show forth its absolute exigence. If the Incarnation cannot incorporate this too, then there will be a whole stage in the history of humanity which must be rejected and a whole section of mankind which is doomed to frustration. To sanctify the individual without sanctifying the social man is labour in vain. Vain *de facto* because clumsy, vain *de jure* because erroneous. Because it is a lack of coherence in the economy of the Redemption; it is to consent implicitly in blocking the law of the Incarnation. What does it matter to me if I am elevated and sanctified in myself, in my person, in my sensibility, my passions, my work, and my wealth if all that is contributed by me and my works to the social life is from the outset dead and formless matter. There precisely is the danger of my being most miserable, for the whole of my being is penetrated and shot through with social life.

Thus the Christian, far from seeing the permanent presence of the community and the common good as an obstacle to his personal perfection, will rejoice in it as a broadening and assuring influence, since this "socialness" is the matter and the instrument of incarnation. The more the common good is woven into the warp and woof of social life, to that extent will there be eminent matter for grace, and it will be, if one can say it thus, the soil of the Mystical Body—not an agglomeration of individuals but a community of men in the deepest sense of the word.

So we are quite ready to acclaim the grandeur of the social and communitarian aspirations which have traversed the nineteenth century and which exalt the minds of the twentieth; for we see in it a magnificent field of work for Christianity; the flowering of apostolates, specialised according to the different functions of men in society, is in truth the beginning of the cultivation of this field; it is the mystical incorporation of Christ in the community life of man.

The social duties of a Christian are thus seen, not as something superadded, but as a necessary condition, though external and accidental, of his Christian life; these duties are in Christ the very law of perfection.

We conclude with Pope Pius XI: Catholic Action is not something exterior to the Christian, it is the very rule of his life.

Catholic Action

Now let us look at Catholic Action. We can see it in its true context; not only its theoretical context but its origin and source in practice; it is right in the midst of contemporary social effervescence, resisting the laicising of social institutions and of the whole framework of society. Thus it grows, requiring of every Christian not merely the sanctification of himself personally but also of his milieu, the sphere in which he lives.

There was once a time when the Christians recoiled before the magnitude of these social phenomena, especially those of the world of labour where machinism had rendered more sensible and more pressing this new collectivism; and so they withdrew into a fearful seclusion. They were frightened by the anti-Christian (or a-Christian) force of these social structures, and attempted, more or less consciously, the experiment of sanctifying the individual against the social structures which, in reality, made up their life, even going so far as to condemn these structures as being responsible for all misdeeds. For a long time, far too long, magnificent apostolic zeal was spent in 'protecting' the Christian from his milieu, and in creating for him an artificial milieu where he could take refuge and at last live a Christian life, in a closed group far from pagan and perverse influences. At some given moment this was perhaps the inevitable last resource, but its strict empiricism would lead us to a Christianity of exiles, cut off from life, from the realities of their daily life, from their status and classes; to a Christianity without grip or audacity, to a Christianity which was disincarnated, that is to say without incarnation, abandoning the condemned and confounded mass of paganised humanity to its misery. This was more than an error of tactics; it was a structural fault because it was an error of doctrine. It attempted to set the religious psychology of these men over against the very matter of their existence, as though the Christian life was not one with the laborious content of their human life and could only subsist by barricading itself against this labour which was incapable of redemption and joyful sanctity. It was a sin against the reality of the Incarnation.

As a result of this defensive attitude with its spiritual protectionism there was a grave risk of losing the spirit of conquest and of reducing the apostolate to 'good works'. What is the use of the yeast if it is not put into the mass? that hard and heavy mass of the real; human life of the earthly proletariat which is us all. In a word, Christianity or the apostolate became an activity more and more reserved to priests, as though the apostolate was not the normal radiation of every Christian as such, as though Christians could live otherwise than in society, fully in society. Catholic Action is the restoration of this apostolic sense in the Christian soul. It is the yeast thrust once more into the middle of the mass. It is the divine life elevating the whole of human life without rejecting anything, the Incarnation continued in the

Mystical Body of Christ. Work, business, firms, trades, offices: everything must be brought into the Christian life. The whole of human civilisation is the subject matter of Christianity. So when the Catholic layman is called to participate in the hierarchical apostolate of the Church (that is the official, quasi-canonical, definition of Catholic Action), it is not to make up for the numerical insufficiency of the clergy nor to help with the extra work caused by new organisations. No, their participation is an essential law of the life of the Church, a law which has existed from the beginning but whose importance and demands are being revealed to the full in modem times. Its repeated promulgation by Pope Pius XI, at every possible opportunity, will stand out as a leading date in the history of Christendom: the recognition by the Church of the social demands of the Christian life in each of her members. Catholic Action is the means whereby the Mystical Body (*cf* section 2 of this article) attains its fullness in the social life of man (*cf* section 1).

But note well that it is not a question of organisation; as one sometimes hears, it is the extension and the strengthening of the tactics of the apostolate by organisations which are better adapted. It is a question of human substance in which the Incarnation must be accomplished, since it is the whole man who must be saved by incarnation. It is concerned with a spirit (a mystique) of the presence of the Spirit brooding over the waters of this new human world; and beginning from this spirit it deals with problems of structure and not merely with the aptness or otherwise of certain *tactics* of approach of modern Christianity.

The true structure of Christendom is before us in the form of the apostolate of 'specialised' movements, for they are precisely the appropriate means for incarnating the divine life in the milieu of the labourer, the farmer, the student, the sailor, the employer and the financier. They do not, under pretext of sanctifying themselves, level out the values which are proper to their profession, or to their state of life, for the human substance of these milieux form the watersheds whence they draw the resources of their work.

Social physique and social morality differ from that of individuals and of families, the former is not merely the extension of the latter but is quite a new dimension in the structure of humanity—this Aristotle had already observed and noted in his divisions of the domains of morality. It is the same for the apostolate, for Catholic Action is not an enlargement of an already existing technique. It does not add lay curates to a clergy which is numerically below strength, but rather, coming from the very essence of the Kingdom of God and from the inmost nature of the Church, it is an extension of the Incarnation to a new social regime which is to arise in Christendom. This extension will be brought about by new apostolic structures which will be complementary but also necessary and urgent and of which Pius XI has given the regulating principle: the participation of the laity in the hierarchical apostolate of the Church.

This apostolate of the laity in the Church, working in Catholic Action, will arise to the extent that the streams of human life take on this social aspect which we have noted, and to the extent that these streams are infused into the supernatural tissue of Christendom. Consequently one can exclude from direct participation in Catholic Action those groups which care for the individual ascetical progress of their members, those which are concerned with the practice of piety, the apostolate of prayer, the exercise of charity in all its forms. These are all undoubtedly good works, full of supernatural graces and of benefits for the individual and social apostolate, but their immediate end is not to incarnate the life of grace in their social milieux and in those social institutions which are the proper object of this evangelisation.

In the same way, an association formed to defend the liberty of Catholics in civic matters is obviously not as intimately a part of Catholic Action as a group of employers or of workers who take it upon themselves to sanctify their milieu and to be the nucleus of a "state of grace" in their work. The former fulfils an external function of apologetic which in certain circumstances is urgent; but die latter is a section of the interior life of Christendom, of the Mystical Body growing to full stature.

SOURCE: Paul McGuire and John Fitzsimons, *Restoring All Things: A Guide to Catholic Action*, (London: Sheed and Ward, 1939), 1–15. Original unknown and name of the translator is unknown.

InterfaceTheology 7/2 2021

Contributors

Ulrich Engel, OP, is Professor of Philosophical-Theological Boundary Issues at the Philosophisch-Theologische Hochschule Münster, and Director of the Institut M-Dominique Chenu Berlin (Germany).

Janette Patricia Gray, RSM (1952–2016), was an Australian Sister of Mercy who was the first non-Jesuit academic Principal of Jesuit Theological College, Parkville, Melbourne. She was a Senior Lecturer in Theology at the University of Notre Dame Australia, Western Australia 1999–2003, Faculty of Jesuit Theological College, Parkville, Melbourne 2004–2014, Lecturer & Supervisor at the United Faculty of Theology (UFT), Pilgrim College and Yarra Theological Union (YTU) (latterly University of Divinity, Melbourne). Janette was also a member of the National Council of Churches in Australia's (NCCA) Faith and Unity Commission 2013–2016. The piece in this volume is used with permission.

Thomas Franklin O'Meara, OP, grew up in Des Moines, Iowa and Madison, Wisconsin; he is member of the Dominican Order. After doctoral education in Munich, Germany, he taught at Aquinas Institute in Dubuque for thirteen years. During that time he also taught at Wartburg Lutheran Seminary, Boston College, and Ibadan, Nigeria. He was a professor at the University of Notre Dame from 1980 to 2003. Past President of the Catholic Theological Society of America he has authored fifteen books among which are: *Theology of Ministry; Thomas Aquinas Theologian; Vast Universe. Christian Revelation and Extraterrestrials.*